Witch Warriors, Workers

An anthology of contemporary working women's poetry

Edited by
Jane Burn & Fran Lock

I am not free while any woman is unfree,
even when her shackles are very different from my own.

—Audre Lorde

First published in 2020 by **Culture Matters Co-Operative Ltd**.
Culture Matters promotes a socialist and progressive approach to art, culture and politics. See www.culturematters.org.uk

Copyright © the contributors
Cover image: © Jane Burn
Commissioned by **Culture Matters**
Layout and typesetting by Alan Morrison
ISBN 978-1-912710-16-4

Acknowledgements
The support of Unison for this anthology is gratefully acknowledged.

Contents

By Gaslight
Poems of intimacy: its beauties and abuses

The Daily Grind
Poems that reflect the hardships and peculiar moments of happiness to be found in our daily lives

Home
Poems about migration, displacement, exile and belonging

Inside / Outside
Poems that focus on issues of "health", physical and mental

Last Chance for this Earth
Poems relating to our precarious environment

Creed
Poems relating to our spirituality

'Enclosure' by Fran Lock

Introduction

By Fran Lock

What it isn't: anthology as manifesto, anthology as Grand Unified Theory of Women Workers' Art, anthology as some kind of definitive statement, anthology as enclave, anthology as tribe.

What we hope it is: anthology as question, anthology as network, anthology as conversation, anthology as site and occasion for celebration and for grieving. It's about making space, retuning attention, listening. It's about uncovering the hidden affinities between diverse modes of creative practice, between women writing across a broad range of aesthetic dispositions; a spectrum of intellectual and imaginative concerns. There's no house style here. No prescriptive dictates on theme or form, nothing a poem must be or do in order to qualify. We wanted to avoid making the essentialising and highly political value judgements that occasionally—perhaps inevitably—creep into the editing of poetry anthologies. We don't want to valorise accessibility and emotionality on the one hand, or materiality and game play on the other. We're interested in particularity and polyphony, in variety and difference. We hope we've provided a platform for that, and for sharing some powerful and inspiring poetry.

As women we don't celebrate ourselves enough, don't celebrate each other. I think this is particularly true for working-class women. We're told boasting is vulgar, that the blowing of our own trumpet is an unattractive quality. We're told this by people who succeed by default, who garner praise and support as they roll through life on greased castors; who don't know what it is to be impeded or rejected or ignored. These elites don't need to big themselves up, their achievement is assumed: because they're men, because they're white, because they're sedentary, because they're wealthy, because they went to the right university. All or any of the above really, in a variety of equally infernal combinations. To be a working-class woman—hell, to be a woman full-stop—is to exist at a very particular axis of erasure and suppression.

This has been on my mind a great deal since the general election, the results of which can only be described as devastating. And devastating in unique ways for women. We've already seen how Tory immigration policy detains women refugees unfairly and indefinitely in demeaning and dangerous conditions, and how cuts to Child Benefit coupled with restrictions to the access of Legal Aid have trapped women in appalling situations of domestic abuse. Poverty itself is a form of structural violence, embedded in the social systems that administer us, and characterised by pronounced inequalities. Poverty, precarity, and unemployment are absolutely entangled with domestic violence: unemployment in men being often a potential trigger for violent behaviour, and unemployment in women creating a condition of dependency on violent and abusive partners. This last point is particularly depressing, in that women who experience violence are more likely to suffer from a range of mental health issues. We have already seen the damage Tory cuts to mental health budgets have wrought.

The situation is dire, and yet we minimise a lot. The destructive social pressure on working-class men to remain close-lipped and granite-jawed in the face of pain has been—rightly—widely discussed in recent years. It's a real problem, of course, but lest we forget, nobody wants our suffering either. It might be easier for women to talk among themselves, but the wider world, the wider culture, demands of us a ludicrous level of stoicism. The medical profession routinely downplays female specific pain, our mental health issues are seen through the skewing lens of gender, our failure to heal in the face of trauma is treated as a moral fault. Society wants linear trajectories of recovery: from victim to survivor, from sufferer to exemplar of wellness. If we're messy and grieving, if we're unable to reproduce the values and embodied forms demanded of us, we're found wanting, swept under the rug.

Now more than ever we need to stand together and rise against this tendency. Power elites would divide us. They would tell British women they can feel no solidarity with refugee women, that straight and queer women can't stand shoulder to shoulder; that sedentary women and Traveller women are at odds. And we're not. Mainstream culture side-lines our narratives. It does so to stop us talking to each other, to prevent us from listening, from really hearing each other, from coming to an awareness of everything we share. Our art is understood to deal in the domestic or confessional, with a limited interiority that never quite rises above its personal preoccupations. It's as if women artists and poets are in a locked room somewhere, talking to ourselves, squinting through the keyhole at the wider world beyond. This is a bullshit paradigm. And it isn't confession, it's testimony: purposeful and vigorously performative. It is of the world. It is speaking to you.

I like to think the poems in this anthology offer a vision of women's lives, and of feminism that's collective, porous and multiple. That they offer a sorority of mutual responsibility, of duty and of care. That this collection offers some small space of recognition, of ourselves and of each other, as artists and creators. It's somewhere we can listen to one another, but we also believe it represents a vivid, vital contribution to poetry and to culture. A resounding free-form jazz solo on our collective golden trumpet.

8

Nuclear Family
Poems about the complexities of family life

'Matriarchy' *by Natalie Sirett*

"It is a Scots tradition that a woman's wedding china is shared among her daughters. I wonder if this subdivision continues, so that in 20 generations the baby girl inherits a fragment of porcelain, too small to see but nonetheless a connection to her matriarchal line?"

My heart is fraught with many a secret sorrow —
With many a care the world may never know;
I sleep to dream of joy, then comes the morrow,
With hope deferred, wrapped in wreaths of snow.'

—*Ellen Johnston* (1835-1873)

'Hail, beauteous, tender little flower,
Sweet pledge of mutual love,
May gladness gild thy childhood's hour
And sunshine from above;
And blessings on thy head descend,
And gentle Peace, my little friend.'

—*Elizabeth Horne Smith* (1876-?)

'Tis mother that rocks you: lie still, love! lie still!
Or these flounces will never be done;
And there's nothing to eat, little darling, until
I have plaited them on, every one.'

—*Fanny Forrester* (1852-1889)

When my Teenage Son Cries

After all we have been through, you and me.
Those days after your birth — the nearly dead time,
tests and tubes time. I used to pray beside
your plastic cot — *if we can just get through this.*
That time we spent, closeted up — those early years
of finding our feet, our health again
just brought us closer. We have this bond.
You grew so fit and well. It's like that time
belonged to someone else — my reed, my tall,
my gentle, happy boy. I thought at first
it was only this teenage, awkward age
that was making a prisoner of your limbs,
a muffle of your brain. After your diagnosis,
I was brisk — cleared the cupboards of crap,
Googled, got rid of gluten. Promised you
that we would Not Let This Win.
We have tried not to panic, to give way to fear.
Sometimes, when you come back home
I can tell things didn't go well, that your body
let you down again. I make you food, try not
to let you see that I am watching you balance a forkful,
do your best to eat. I can tell by the sunken gloom
beneath your eyes, the bruised smudge around them.
The lines that crease your sockets — lines that last year,
you did not have. There are so many griefs
but none have hurt me more so far than seeing
those teardrops track your downturned face.
I have always done my best to tell you that it's okay
to cry. I sit next to you and touch your hand.
You lay your head in my lap and break your heart.

Jane Burn

Fucking Snails

/ shitting babies
in the weeds again / *mummy*
it's a little green one, I seed it /
how many times / do I have
to tell you / I've seen / or I
saw? / are you deaf or just /
stupid? / the pathetic dramas
when I snuff them with a pinch /
it's best / to kill them before
they get too big / untameable /
her hair curls like parsley /
round and round the table
with the hairbrush / screaming /
I made porridge / the right way
like my mum / salt and water /
why won't she sit still
and take it?

Kirsten Luckins

His autism in the power of rain

We cowered in the kitchen from the rainthreat.
As a glowered sky grumbled on Angus, we
cosied, cupped our comfort of tea, bit buttered scones.
     Heaven ripped. We lost him.
Lost him for a million terrifies of seconds —

found him. Found him out in that Kirrie garden, danced

by the hard rain, stung-skinned on his seven year
naked of self, drenched in the joy of storms,
laughed happy. Wild in flashed lightning, he spun

joys our dried-out flesh still missed.

Beth McDonough

First published by Rainy Fiction (April 2014), and subsequently in *Handfast*

A Birth Journey in Nine Movements

We are *en route* to Yorkshire.
I stir my latte with a pregnancy test,
it shows up positive,
all the waiters do the *Macarena*.
My mother finds a *Clear Blue* box in the fridge —
it is full of eggs.
We have omelette for tea.
The family has never been so together.

I am carried around by four angels
who guard my apple pip cargo,
pump me full of oxytocin,
airbrush the stretch marks.

My body wages war on vegetables,
organic and tinge of green are off the menu.
I am possessed by the *Honey Monster*,
only pear drops and jelly tots will do.

Three weeks to go and somebody has let the bath out —
Oligohydramnios. The midwife tells me you're shrinking.
The sofa becomes a wet grave I bury myself in.

The hospital — I have a bed with a bell,
Mr Doc says emergency caesarean.
We float round the room like balloons in denial.
Seven days go by — you are still not out,
despite Doctor Patel's insistence,

despite the letter on serious yellow paper,
despite my dangerously high blood pressure.
I sense we are dying. I am probed silence.
You have been leaked information.
You are not coming.

C-section. They find you. I become *Mummy*.

The room breathes morphine, the women sweat.
I am in *Tenko*. The nurse has a moustache.
She withholds pain relief, wheels away precious baby.
A cold star rises above the saline drip,
guards the broken nativity.

My old skin lines the corridor,
the curt nurse picks it up.
Strangely, I cry because you are no longer inside.
Your dad closes the curtain in case they think I am depressed.
I'm not. It's just that I will never again know such intimacy.

Michelle Diaz

form ever follows function

unpadded kneelers and a framed poem on the shrine wall for saint margaret clitherow pressed to death on lady day good friday her zeal led her to harbour spread out on the ground sharp stone at her back pray for us

amenorrhea

Did she have children? Or was faith her focus?

oh England thy fruit in the fields in the trees rotting thy work and pensions pressed on borrowed time wrong word stollen sugar and butter this year foreign merry christmas surge in spending drone takedown pray for us

amenorrhea

Yes, but did she have her own children?

des corps fatigués des mains fatiguées des dos broyés des regards épuisés (édouard louis) pathetic even tragic commentary on life as it is ordinarily lived (john dewey) pressed you will get two breaks the cage will open automatically step out pray for us

amenorrhea

So are you going to have kids or what?

sedimentary suffering which ground where doesn't matter arms wide open hands open for rain in the grave not like jesus risen up there's got to be some other hands down there to touch tiny morsels of flesh and bone left underground an archaeological dig cordoned off pray for us

amenorrhea

Evidence of prior pregnancy?

writing religion they will come for me she was seen in chapels with relics eyeing clitherow's hand

in a bell jar she was seen in sacré coeur that dreadful basilica atonement for la commune there are good guys and bad guys and she was definitely sitting there next to a trump voter she was weeping at the sight of people weeping at the sight of the sacrament at—one—ment which war are we fighting now anyway which bot the usage at the time 1586 at—one—ment no doubt

amenorrhea

Does she have children? Does she confess it in writing?

Kimberly Campanello

The Turning Point

I try to explain the world I came from
to my children, because it was a different one to
this, and not just in the sense that every generation
believes the world they grew up in
to be better than their children's. I tell them
about a house without carpet or wallpaper,
because we were poor, about the dole office
and having to get the bus everywhere
and not having a landline or colour TV. Being poor
is not something they understand. This makes me
equally glad and worried. I tell them about a world
without internet, Netflix, YouTube, fifty brands of biscuits
and ice cream at the supermarket which, back then,
was tiny and only open eight hours a day. I tell
them about the bliss of waiting for my favourite
programmes to come on. They ask if I was born
in Roman times. They ask what I mean by 'no internet'.
I tell them about having no mobile phone,
or even a landline, which meant that you went
outside and knocked on friends' doors if you wanted
to play, or you'd arrange to meet up by the city hall
or the market at noon on Saturday and if one of you
couldn't make it the other would just have to stand there
and work it out. I tell them I hadn't heard of
climate change, or tacos, or gelato, or avocado
and I had no idea we were poor, not really. I tell them
having no internet meant I couldn't Google symptoms
or addresses or look up someone's online profile,
I didn't spend bus journeys scrolling Instagram

or watching movies but staring out the window or writing
and yes, I was bored often, I was muddy and bloodied
often, I was hindered and poor and cat-called and groped
and it was illegal for married women to work
it was illegal to be gay or have an abortion and I watched
a black friend get punched and called names I don't repeat
and I too was called names for being Irish.
In my street a family was kicked out of
their home for being Catholic, and every July a bonfire
would be built at the top of our street from wooden crates.
Everyone got drunk and the flames melted the windows.
I heard bombs go off often. We were searched often.
Every year the Arctic ice shrank and returned. We
ate blackberries in October. Each winter,
winter came. Bottled water didn't exist.
There were less than ten thousand pieces
of plastic in the ocean and the Amazon
had not been stripped down to raw nerve and its million
species thrived in a colourful blaze, loud and diverse.
We were politically ravaged but hopeful.
The checkpoints faded, the border patrol
died away. On the other side of the world the twin
towers were built, like something Kubrick imagined,
and the Great Barrier Reef bloomed,
a living rainbow. I tell them
that we talked about the Holocaust in the
context of a one-off, of course it was a one-off, the
absolute bowels of human atrocity and tyranny,
a consequence of *us* and *them*
that taught us all, didn't it, taught us not

to hate, at least not that much. My children
tell me that I was rich, for that flawed
and often terrible world did not have oceans
containing fifty trillion pieces of plastic, for that
sexist and racist and homophobic world held its leaders
to account, that dumb world
had not yet wilfully blinded itself, erased its own memory clean,
it was a world
at the turning point
> of the human race,
> the point at which we had a sense of
> what could still be lost and how we might
> yet
> turn back.

Carolyn Jess-Cooke

The Pickle Woman

for Mairead Miller

When the woman behind
the trolley half-full

of jarred, whole
dill pickles approaches

the desk, asks whether there
are more to be had,

and in the shift
of her body you discern

a fully distended belly,
it is only left to wonder

whose craving it is:
mother, fetus, or

this transient, third self.

Carrie Etter
Originally published in *The Broadsheet*

any mother's sons

with eyes the inconclusive blue of institution
windows. eyes unfocussed. boys with puzzled
buttonholes. boys in plimsolls, kitchen haircuts,
silver thighs like tinned sardines. the scutty
hedges, *thick with 'em.* boys in navy blazers.
grim fringes, pigeon chests. boys with unsigned
plaster casts, the bitten lips of injured pride.
all acned swagger, baccy burns. the taciturn
and bantam boys, who flail their clustered
featherweight. live off dread and shredded
wheat, grinding their teeth in the d minus
dark. the washers of bottles, collectors
of cans, the stretchers-out of errand. boys
who store their fathers' habits in their hands.
rabbit skinners, buriers of wrans. boys, on
cunning occasions: green eye so sly it slides
right off a face. violated in triplicate. applying
at the barracks to be formally concussed. who
have their feet gauged for leather coffins.
boys who wear the ragged sleeves of grief,
and drag their cuffs through butter. boys,
with acrimonious nosebleeds, bearing
their seasick mouths before. swinging shirtless
from the monkey bars, stretching freckles into
melanoma. boys who chance the bisecting
light of building sites, soft-mouthing your
secrets like labrador dogs. sepal and beguiled
inside their hoods. or uniformed scarecrows,
crucified. their arms collect the silhouettes
of birds. whose *smiles* break like flocks
of birds. corvid ephemera, raving.
pocketers of apple cores, of endless blank
revisioning. with eyes turned down against

the blue promissory window. fallacy
and forfeit, a kind of stooped bravura.
boys with limbs you cut from snares.
whose laugh is rubber into skin. at
closest range. whose laughter's made
by sweeping up stray echoes from
a stairwell. boys, doing lateral minded
handstands up a prison wall. in
an embarrassment of streamers: black.
who broke their cagey strut on stones.
we set them down on sateen. boys
with softened edges. boys wrapped
up in pale blue tissue. boys reduced to
milk teeth, trainers; shrines and flags.
boys we cling more firmly to each day.
whose faces are medals, pinned by green-
gold ribbon. whose bodies are slender
projectiles. fixed to the fatigued heart.

Fran Lock

Leavings

The devils and the lunatics are loose;
bear your children, keep them close

at first. Weave a cocoon of hair and skin,
a silver song to grow them in.

Raise them naked as the angels, sweet
and safe; but mix their milk with grit.

Fold them in love and gift them ear and tongue
that they might parley with anyone.

Teach them courage, how to rise and focus.
Muscle them like little boxers.

Wait for it: those fists and minds will soon
turn quicker than your own,

will read this world, will try to cuff or kiss it,
will ask you —*you*— how to fix it.

Shrug; then spin this orb, this creaking prize,
spread out the maps, the changing lines,

throw up your wrinkled hands, unveil the wreck
you've left them: the fires, the slow black,

the cleft and spill. Confess: *this bruised world, blue
and plundered; now it belongs to you.*

Jacqueline Saphra
Originally Published in *All My Mad Mothers* (Nine Arches Press, 2017)

Union

You arrived, an idea in a knitted hat and mittens
packed in a box on the kitchen table.

We forgot about you and were startled
by your voice, wrecking our schedule,

testing our laissez faire arrangements,
demanding hands-on improvisation

with night feeds, nappies, holding, rocking,
pushing, undressing, washing, a factory line

of endless needs. You were Foreman,
we the tired labourers who struggled

against the shocking hours and work conditions
as we watched the clock for the end of the shift

that never came.
But you paid us in love and we became rich.

Ellen Phethean

Rural Graft
Poems exploring our relationships to landscape and to nature through the prism of labour

Image by Mary Lou Springstead

'The wicked who would do me harm
May he take the disease,
Globulary, spirally, circularly,
Fluxy, pellety, horny-grim.

Be it fiercer, fiercer, sharper, harder, more malignant,
Than the hard, wound-quivering holly,
Be it sourer than the sained, lustrous, bitter, salt salt,
Seven seven times.'

—*Isabella Chisholm (1865-1882)*

'The brave knights on the moor when the grouse are a-drive,
Slay so many, you'd think there'd be none left alive;
Oh! The desperate daring of slaughtering grouse,
Can only be matched in a real slaughterhouse.'

—*Marion Bernstein (1846-1906)*

'When a gilpy o' nine, I was set doon to wark
At the auld spinnin' wheel, an' frae morning till dark
I spun, for my mither was thrifty and snell,
An' wadna alloo me to jauk or rebel.'

—*Janet Hamilton (1795-1873)*

'There's chappin' an' clippin' an' sawin' o' airn;
Burnin' and sotterin', reengin' an' knockin';
Scores o' puir mortals roastin' and chokin'.
Gizzene'd and dry ilka thrapple and mouth,
Like cracks in the yird in a het simmer drought...'

—*Janet Hamilton (1795-1873)*

This Land is Our Land: Towards a Working-Class Rural Feminism

By Fran Lock

Idyllic, now there's a word I could happily live without ever hearing again. *Idyllic!* in the effusive, as applied by settled, city friends to my rural childhood. Or, rather, to their mental image of it, which, to say the least, is somewhat unrealistic. Don't misunderstand me, I loved—still love—the lonely windswept landscapes of my youth, but not without ambivalence, not without pain; not without an intimate understanding of all their *idyll* comes at the expense of.

There's a disconnect, you see, a failure of cultural imagination. For the urban middle-classes the countryside figures as a scene of utopian escape. They haven't lived there, they don't know, the way they think is wrong: as if the city and the country were entirely separate spheres; as if the rural were an alien, autonomously functioning world, its mode of life predicated upon economic principals and cultural values far beyond the average city-dweller's ken. They don't perceive, because they don't allow themselves to perceive, the entangled causal relationships between the urban and the rural; the complex dynamics of hierarchy, erasure and suppression in which they themselves are enmeshed. Media discourses fuel this blindness, promoting the image of the countryside as an infinitely accessible leisure space, a picturesque resource to be tapped by the affluent. The notion of escape is critical here. If the idea of the rural is aligned in middle-class imagination with a flight from the pressures of city-living, it is also a site of abdication from social responsibility; an effectively depoliticised zone, in which spatial and moral separation from one's broader community are conflated and confused.

Idyllic has come to stand for a place of recreation and ease. When its original meaning is evoked, the rural work it envisages tends towards the nostalgic, or the romantically valorised cottage industry, that happy province of a middle-class diaspora who *gave it all up* for a *simpler way of life*. Never mind that such quaint home-grown businesses constitute a toothless performance of the trades that gentrification has supplanted and made non-viable. Never mind that the countryside is anything but *simple*. As for *giving it all up* as being somehow uniquely virtuous or heroic, what an absolute and arrant crock. Renunciation is a choice, a choice made freely and with full economic agency; a choice made within a network of supports and resources—financial, logistical and social—that most rural working-class people simply do not have.

So yes, I dislike the term *idyllic*, it obscures more than it describes. Nevertheless, in an anthology of in an anthology of women workers' poetry poetry, it is appropriate to consider its roots, how the idyll form traditionally focussed on intimate portrayals of rural life, and the tactile relationship rural workers had with their trades. This matters because nowhere, to my mind at least, is the intersection between embodied experience and labour more legible and more fraught than in the daily lives and hidden histories of women.

It has always struck me as curious that the westernised imagination—and indeed much research—has traditionally held such a limited conception of the lives and concerns of rural women, tending to reinforce conservative expectations of women's roles in the home and community: a *supporting* or *subordinate* role as wives and mothers. Notions of rural masculinity, meanwhile, are predicated upon human mastery over environment. Remote or hostile landscapes encourage the construction and valorisation of a masculinity associated with power, physical strength and mental ingenuity. Frequently, men are pitched, in work and in leisure, as *doing battle* with nature; one succeeds as a man if one defeats the forces of nature through the application of bodily strength and courage.

Mastery is capitalism's shtick too. The rhetoric runs that the natural world is a resource, ripe for exploitation. Farm and other resource-based labour reinforces traditional masculinity through its emphasis on bodily strength, and in the ways it associates skill and success with physical prowess. You don't attempt to live in rhythm with your environment, you conquer and subdue it, beat it into submission. And if your environment is the enemy, you need have no compunction about the way you treat it, pillage and despoil it; no qualms about your responsibility to it. Mastery breeds deforestation and battery farming. Mastery is endless and ultimately untenable, expansion.

Mastery has had its day. It is no longer viable. We're living in a time of unprecedented ecological crisis. We need desperately to inaugurate a new model of environmentally conscious stewardship. Capitalism doesn't want to admit this, and so capitalism peddles the same old, tired, patriarchal crap in its portrayal of rural people, rural trades, and agricultural labour: The Farmer is a Man. And if the male body is the site and source of expertise, technical control, and power, then the female body is site and source of what exactly? There's a bit of biologically determinist quackery here: the female body is aligned to the land, to its rhythms and cycles. Rural women are *closer to nature*, by which is meant we breed, we mother, we nurture, we embody all the fertile feminine virtues. And if rural women are *closer to nature*, and if nature is something to be dominated and mastered, then doesn't that make us something to be dominated and mastered also?

Enough. We need to look and think again about what it means to be a woman in a rural environment, engaged in rural labour, rural trades. Because we *do* exist in an intimate and tactile relationship to the land. Not in a vague, romanticised way, wafting around the moors in inappropriate cheesecloth a la Kate Bush doing 'Wuthering Heights'. And not in a passive and subordinate way. Our engagement with our environment is, rather, practical and active, and uniquely pressured. To be a working-class woman in a remote rural location is to understand to the ounce, how far you can stretch a bag of flour. It's knowing how to grow things, when to plant and when to reap, how to wire your own plugs, fix your own sink. And it's knowing this stuff, not because you *want* to, not as a hobby or a pastime, but because that's how you live, how you fill in the gaps created by economic disparity and a chronic lack of access to essential services. Being a working-class woman in the country is also feeding your family in the face of rising unemployment; it's taking whatever shitty, soul-destroying job there is going because that's what you need to survive. It's a fourteen-hour shift at an all-night garage. It's the way the middle-class influx sneer at you, it's living on the sharp edge of both gentrification and climate change. It's lonely, and it's hard.

Yet knowing how to survive with less, how to stretch what you have, how to live responsibly, sustainably, within your environment, this way of living must be our future, *all* our futures. Rural feminism is a feminism that acknowledges women as the vanguard in a radical reimaging of how we interact with the natural world. It is also a feminism that credits the particularity of our practical skills, not homogenising and diminishing them under the broad catch-all of *domesticity*. Rural feminism is ecologically conscious feminism, not feminism as an academic or intellectual exercise. It is a feminism that recognises our resilience—not as a cop-out, a way for the systems that beset us to abdicate responsibility—but something we have to offer, to teach, something we have the right to be proud of.

The countryside is not some utopian *idyll*, it is a complex, political place. The women who inhabit it are complex political agents. They are also joyous, determined, vigilant, and strong.

Hunt Kennels at Bilsdale

An island of hell, eaten into the moor —
a stonewalled secret. You would never know
it was there, would never guess what was caged
inside. You might hear the distant call of ghosts —
a spook's wail at the moon, a notion of haunting
as you hiked past. I was taken to see the hounds
in their kennels —this, I was told, was a treat.
Can you love horses and not follow the hunt?
This was the silent question— the unspoken surmise
that I must. For why else would I have come?
The reek before the sight —excrement, rain-damp pelts,
raw meat. I was just a kid, did not know what to think
about their writhing bodies splotched with tan,
the noise they made. The way they scrabbled the bars
and shoved out their noses made them seem to crave
the friendliness of hands. *Don't touch.* Everywhere,
the smell of bones, their vivid tongues, the wrongness
of their job. The wagon with the winch for fallen stock
waiting for the call to foundered cob, worried sheep,
pneumoniac cow. After, in the farmhouse I was given
cheese on fruitcake. Coming from a dead-pit village,
I had never mouthed that fusion before. It tasted of raisins
and feet. I ate it to be polite, kept my boots on indoors
and nobody yelled. The walls were covered in portraits
of winners in red rosettes, of each other snapped
in mid-audacious leap. I did not understand their world
of byre and grass —this passion for blood, their urge
for death. Their pens of murder-bred dogs.

Jane Burn
First published in *The Poet's Republic*

Homecoming

rivered like trout there's this flash lad
on his hoss
spading hooves

his waterway gymkhana
deep as a tall mare

banks hooked on pebbled gaits

as he drowns thunder with heels
cannon bones firing

two fingers up to the council
distant reivers

hair slicked back
no saddle all bridle

then stomach laid to withers
curb chains drape into her mane

as he speaks in private of diving

for a spell

and ear-close they go under

pressed into the anvil black
sunk like a stone

'til a bubble breaks
then a hand or an ear

he crests
stood on the mirror of himself

barefoot and dripping
in black-wet denim

all teeth and chest shining

half-boy
half-hoss

all bray

Jo Clement

Daljit Nagra and Jo Shapcott selected 'Homecoming' as the Faber runner-up in the Troubadour International Poetry Competition 2018.

Swaling on Boscathow

The farmer tosses purple moor grass into the air —
An Easterly— we're ready to burn.
Pale grey puffs become a bonfire guy legging it
through gorse and bracken. The fire doesn't burn
into the ground, is all surface and speed.
I'm responsible for my patch but if the wind were to run
away, I'd sprint this grassy corridor
or be sacrificed to some god I've yet to hear of.

Annie asks me what to do
as if I've worked a fire this size before.
The contractor, who set the fire,
would be handsome on a film set. Here,
he's in frayed red t-shirt, hole-ridden overalls
open to the groin. I like that he says *he*
instead of the English-English *him* —
I've worked with he before.

The fire finds its own voice, stalls,
worries at a tussock before lurching on.
A shrew bolts. The fire leaves
part of itself, teasy as an orange baby,
writhing by my boots. I do my job and whack it.
The farmer nods —*almost done.*
We breathe in the distant danger,
paraffin rides the air.

Katrina Naomi

First published in *Finished Creatures*

'a song to rest the tired dead'

i.m. Celia Lane

it is dusk
she has come to wash the body
a table is set by the bed
a bowl of lavender water
clean muslin cloths
a white towel
    'too young for death'
she thinks as she removes all the clothing
and jewelry from the body of her niece
she notices stretch marks on the thighs
how the breasts have dropped
from feeding the chavies
    'forty years ago, just been borned
sucking at her Daya's breast.'

taking a cloth
she dips it in water
squeezes it hard in her hand
sets about her task

malts stand by the door way
aunts, daughters, sisters and the daya
singing in low soft voices
a song to rest the dead

she speaks quietly
to her loved one as she gently cleans
lifting one arm up then the other
holding it
placing it down carefully

as if it was made of glass
the others won't move too close
it is mokkadi to do so
this woman who washes the dead
now holds both feet
letting them rest for a while
blessing them for all the miles
they have trod the earth
she dresses her niece in the finest of clothes
combs her dark tangled hair
places the gold chain and earrings in the palm
of the right hand
puts the wedding ring back on
the third finger of the left hand
    'such small fingers'
bending forward, kisses them
   'you are ready now my gel, sov well'

Raine Geoghegan

Romani words (jib):
Chavies — children; Daya — mother; Malts — women;
Mokkadi — unclean; Sov — sleep.

Previously published online at *Here Comes Everyone* (the Rituals Edition, 26/10/18)
& featured on *Poethead* (24/03/19).

Songs For Lesser Gods

1.

Only after the fleece was stripped and rolled,
could we see the jagged bonecrate of one ewe,
each rib half bolted, the knobbled spine askew,
pouched belly swinging low, the fleshless fold
of barren udder. I prized at her reluctant mouth.
Teeth still there mainly, abraded now to grains
from years spent cropping pasture thinned by rain
and summer storms.
                            The God of Broken Mouths
has come for her, pulls up her blue grey tongue
to see the calloused gums, the yellow stubs
emerging from her worn out jaw like insect grubs,
"She'll be pushing up, not eating, daisies soon."

Not yet.
            She joins the shearlings by the wall
But the God of Broken Mouths will have them all.

2.

The hoof, deformed, infected, curled around
like dried up, faded leather from the quick,
the panting, acquiescent ewe lay stoic
as I unsheathed the knife to lance the wound.
A squeamish medic, with gritted teeth, I drained
the abcess of its milky pus and blood,
nauseated by the filthy, putrid flood,
the stench —my stomach flipped, the fat ewe strained,
kicked me full on in churning abdomen
thrashed wildly, connecting with my cheek— in shock

I loosed my grip, she bolted for the flock,
her lameness gone. The breeze whispered 'Amen.'
The God of Thankless Tasks, patron of ewes,
in battered pride and bruises claims his dues.

3.

The God of Lambs and Sleepless Nights is back;
another shift out by the stockyard wall
where ewes are gathered, sheltering from the squall,
the blizzard and the blackout.
                          At dawn's first crack
I'm dragged to watch them loosening the weight
of heavy lambs in ones and twos and threes,
the slop of life, the sweaty, bloodstained seas
spout through the bloated womb's oppressed sluice-gate.
Most shed their loads with little help from me,
half-hearted midwife, hankering for my bed,
here shivering, playing shepherdess instead,
arms naked, soaped in readiness to free
the stuck or stubborn, the vital or stillborn
to the God of Lambs and Sleepless Nights I'm sworn.

4.

The fat man of the moon leans on the night,
shakes off the clouds and rests a steadfast gaze
across this vacant valley. The autumn blaze,
slow rust of leaves, a fire-flow of light
gleams on the grassy flanks of silent fields.
A red-gold streak, the burnished dart of fox
glints and is gone —the ghosts of vanished flocks
stir with the breeze. A fallow deer, concealed

in brush and briar, skims the gritstone wall,
careers along the empty, twisting lane,
from dark to light to dark.
                    The valley's pain
drifts from the hills, an anguished, deathly pall.

The God of Plague has seeded every field,
the lesser gods must bow their heads and yield.

Lesley Quayle

Body Politic
Poems that engage the contested territories of women's bodies

Image by Jane Burn

There were female chiefs in the Cabinet,
(Much better than males I'm sure!)
And the Commons were three-parts feminine,
While the Lords were seen no more!

—Marion Bernstein (1846-1906)

'Wanted a husband who doesn't suppose,
That all earthy employments one feminine knows,–
That she'll scrub, do the cleaning, and cooking, and baking,
And plain needlework, hats and caps, and dressmaking.
Do the family washing, yet always look neat,
Mind the bairns, with a temper unchangeably sweet,
Be a cheerful companion, whenever desired,
And contentedly toil day and night, if required.
Men expecting as much, one may easily see,
But they're not what is wanted, at least, not by me.'

—*Marion Bernstein (1846-1906)*

'Young women...I trust that the night of your ignorance...as a class, is far spent, and that the day is at hand in which you will give earnest and devoted application to the many means of mental improvement...The right use of these will place you in a position to cast off the works of darkness and assume that armour...which is your defence and your glory.'

—*Janet Hamilton on the Education of Women, Poems, Essays, and sketches, 1880.*

So, I Grabbed Ahold of My Own Cunt

Better that than under the thumb of the wrong man.
The one that shits a brick cos your hemline's above the knee,
the one who sights a level with your breasts.
Come, you upskirters,
    gropers,
    fiddlers.
Roll up, roll up to where we're stuck,
behind our desk, our till, our bar, our counter top, our stall.
Come,
with moisture on your smacking lips, rub keen palms
on greasy fabric thighs.
Bless us and our pursefuls of pin money, shackled
to your trouser pocket rummaging for change,
your come-to-bed conversation, leaning that bit over,
catch
a sneaky treat of tit, a clue of cleft. Here, you say,
as we kneel to stack a shelf. *While you're down there, pet.*
Look how we break the day around our babies,
bite our tongues
or get the boot.
Look how the bags-for-life have have swung
their weighted lacerations on our skin.
Watch us
check behind before we bend, sense you fix the open target,
thrust with the intrusion of your eyes.
Look at the glass ceiling, how we drown beneath it,
ice over a pond.
How you fear the witch that bleeds five days
and doesn't die,
how we'll only mutter on about *down below*, ask for time off
when our kids are ill. How we'll only cry.
Look how my hand closes a fist, opens like a rose.
Look how we stop going out cos we're sick

of midnight coercion whining up our legs, sniffing out the hole,
the pissed-up booze fumes tongued along our necks.
Listen to your songs — your *I know you want it*,
your justification of *blurred lines.*
I do not want the feel of you inside of me
and so I grabbed ahold of my own cunt
to save you a job,
to save me having to run.

Jane Burn

Lyrics taken from *Blurred Lines*, sung by Robin Thicke

Armlock Number 3

In real life, no-one will stab you overarm
like Norman Bates in *Psycho*,
but we train the move with knives
and bottles, plastic over steel or glass.

You move in, meet the wrist before it's straight,
step forward like a hieroglyph
and force them back and down,
arm concertina'd at the elbow.

This will not break bone,
but wrenches tendons,
leaves the body prone
for kicks or stomps

or what you want. I know
because I had it done to me
by a woman I was crushing on
in my jiu-jitsu class.

Her name was Tanya,
and she didn't mean to hurt me,
not exactly, but the counter
to this move is doing it first,

which is what I failed to do
on the night we were graded,
a night Tanya couldn't hold back.

I couldn't lift a beer with my right hand
for weeks. And every time I tried,
I thought of her.

Ana McKenna

The Trouble with Toy-boys

Bloody Hell, you don't look it
so I kept on not looking it.

But my body knows different.
Macular degeneration
says the casual optician,
but I'll be independent,
able to get around seeing
only what's at the edges.

Ischaemic changes
in the left vessel of the brain
pronounces the neurologist
pointing at a blur
on the MRI scan
while checking his watch.

Gallstones — small to medium
and the bored technician
wipes off the cold gel
with a paper towel
and turns his back
to tap something onto a screen.

CKD says the GP,
that triumphant conjuror.
I faint in the street,
my heart, which I thought
I'd given to you,
banging like a trapped bird.

Carole Bromley

First published in *Yaffle Anthology*

poetry reading

(from *trauma: the opera*)

and for you, my darling/ my high priest of pious pornography/ poetry pimp/ you may fuck my Soho-pink sacred heart// I want to write a book in which I live/ a story where the girl gets the girl/ and the girl is herself/ a novel where I return/ to find a six year old child opening a bedroom door/ and I shotgun, don't do that/ stop all that opera/ there is still so much to learn/ but how do I write/ that if war is God's way of teaching Americans geography/ then maybe this 'this'/ this oh god/ o-god/ is God's way of teaching woman history/ how do I ask her to lift skin/ organise dust/ pin back the night/ excavate/ glue// I know that/ if you press your ear against my shell/ you will hear Bangkok/ my Koh San Road/ or the itch of Moss Side pavements/ the call of corner boys/ slouching, with bees in their mouths// tonight you will hear reindeer over Rotherham/ children/ my mother's funeral laugh/ you will hear black women/ teaching/ scratching chalk outlines on blackboard skin/ unpicking acronyms by candlelight/ my shell sings the sirens of Mount Sinjara/ my song seduces war/ listen/ can you hear a child ticking/ the slow-dance of bones beside Phnom Penn brothels/ my dropped vase/ kintsugi cunt/; paint all the scars in Poundshop glitter, girl// are all women/ inside other women?// & how do I write/ that you are there too/ pretty dust girl/ curled deep in your cave of remarkable horror/ inside yourself/ uroboros/ smiling a no/ putting your headphones on/ staring into your hands/ taking off your fists// every time you/ open your mouth/ a white man jumps out/ and eats you// if war is God's way of teaching Americans geography2/ then maybe rape is God's way of teaching women/ Woman// how do I write that/ there is a grave at the grave meeting of my legs/ & no one goes there after dark/ except with nets to catch all these beautiful ghosts/ pinning them to novels/ pages plucked/ vajazzled// and while we are at it/ how should I write that/ I had all your ghost babies. They live together at the edge of the woods/ and don't write home anymore.

thank you for listening. lay a wreath where the two roads pleat.
photocopy my photograph. return to me once a year. tell them a story.

make me live.

Joelle Taylor

Tampon

I

First to the fight,
small mouse, compact
as a kimono, lozenge
of freedom. A bullet packed within
a body, wound dressing, deliverer
from evil. Throwaway thing, toilet blocker
seaside surprise, stinker, saviour.
Slipper-inner, rip-chord,
parachute, rag for your rag-bag,
stopper-upper, launched
from your pod like a bomb,
coming back swollen and bloated,
a wounded warrior, a freedom fighter.

II

Firstly, disappointment. Where
are the Dalmatians, the roller boots,
the pony tail of sleek, blonde hair
the skin tight body suit?
I expect something to emerge from me
other than blood. I expect a neatness to my
menstruation, not this shameful seep,
the blush each time I sneeze, the clenched thighs.
First time, hovering, one foot
on the bath's white lip. The diagram
is torsoless, a line drawing, a poor man's cunt.
I struggle. I get it wrong, somehow I can't align
my body to its shape. My vagina rejects it.
My body smears its rage in red, across the school nurse's seat.

Wendy Pratt

Dancing the Plank

4am, ward-scuppered with all the other wrecks;
sick and storm-bowed by Cisplatin, salt in your veins.
Cling the rigging of the drip and hoist upright, sway
port to starboard. Build your sea legs.

So, you're dry-docked; mapped with poison
from wrist to elbow: blue anchors of old bruises,
red of heart tattoo. You are still Anne Bonney, Mary Read.
You've not come this far to scrape. Lean

into the swell of your rickety bed: peg-legged,
bilge-breathed, split-mastered. Screw your eye
to the horizon and stagger
this day's plank. Kick up your heels.

Rosie Garland

Six Signs You Might Be a Slattern

Are you a little draggle-tail;
do your skirts bedevil leavings from the gutter?

When you take a turn around the park
do bitches bevy close and claim you kin?

Are you wanton in your daily intercourse,
your ankles grimed, your lips stained cochineal?

And how's your baking lately —
is your dough a coffer for slut's pennies?

Do you hear ill-clamouring in your breast,
is there a midden where your heart should sit?

When a caller raps, does your front door
acquiesce directly, the catch already sprung?

Helen Ivory

First published in *The Anatomical Venus* (Bloodaxe, 2019)

When I Open

When I open my ribs a dragon flies out
and when I open my mouth a sheep trots out
and when I open my eyes silverfish crawl out
and make for a place that's not mine.

When I open my fists two skylarks fly out
and when I open my legs a horse gallops out
and when I open my heart a wolf slips out
and watches from beneath the trees.

When I open my arms a hare jumps out
and when I show you my wrists a shadow cries out
and when I fall to my knees
a tiger slips out and will not answer to me.

Now that the beasts that lived in my chest
have turned tail and fled, now that I'm open
and the sky has come in and left me
with nothing but space, now that I'm ready

to lie like a cross and wait for the ghost
of him to float clear away, will my wild things
come back, will the horse of my legs
and the dragon of my ribs, and the gentle sheep

which lived in my throat, and the silverfish
of my eyes and the skylarks of my hands
and the wolf of my heart, will they all come back
and live here again, now that he's left,

now I've said the word whisper it rape,
now I've said the word whisper it shame,
will my true ones, my wild, my truth,
will my wild come back to me again.

Kim Moore

Previously published in *The North*.

By Gaslight
Poems of intimacy: its beauties and abuses

'Eve Falling' by Natalie Sirett

'Tis better far than thou shouldst live still single
Than married be, in doubts and fears to dwell;
When broken vows within the bosom mingle
It only makes the home a demon's hell.'

—*Ellen Johnston (1835-1873)*

'Now no man could venture to beat his wife,
For the women had settled by law'

—*Marion Bernstein (1846-1906)*

'My hollow eyes burned through a sorrowful mist,
And my forehead no longer was fair,
For a shadow made darker the place he had kissed
For to show that his lips had been there.
O loosened my hair, and I gazed at the wreck,
Till the tears down my faded cheeks rolled;
And I wailed, as those tangled locks swept o'er my neck.
Ah, tresses! Where, where is your gold?

He came to me, dearest, and offered me pay;
But his gold in wild fury I caught,
Declaring, as proudly I hurled it away,
That my *silence should never be bought!*
And had you not nestled so close to my heart,
I had cursed the vile tempter that came,
And made fiercer my hate, when I bade him depart,
By insulting my sorrow and shame.'

—*Fanny Forrester (1852-1889)*

Picture of the Dead Woman as a Bride

She's so thin —hitched to the left, snapped in the middle like a broken
stick. As if she's saying, *I'm sorry. Sorry for being so tall.* It's the seventies,
so her dress is a mix of peasant-milkmaid, Victorian high-buttoned neck
and frill. Her hair is acorn brown, swooped to the side with lacquer.
Her face is scrubbed. She is cradling pink roses as they bud from a mist
of baby's breath. Her clutch on the spray is rigid, veins spindling the back
of her hand. Her elbow-length veil is fixed to her head with a band
of satin flowers —it's too much round her face. It nets her in. Later,
three children will add to her girth but for now, a pearly belt rides
the small circumference of her waist. Her chest looks hollow, scooped
as the breeze drifts through her satin snow. Thirty eight years later,
she killed herself. I know that I am searching her body for clues, trying
to measure her eyes for reasons why. I put my palm over half
of the photograph, blank out the man so I see only her. She is untethered,
floats from the portrait. A rising cloud.

Jane Burn

First published in the *Valley Press Anthology of Prose Poetry*

Some context in mitigation

We like to know when our next meal's coming,
what it'll be, think about tea as we're dishing up
dinner, know pork's superior to beef, how to hide

the crackling for later. We say adding spices
and herbs is mucking about with food, make gravy
properly, from a packet. Our lips are puckered

not from smoking but from judging, one step away
from nothing. We exchange glances when a woman
speaks loudly, are quick to spot a lack of knickers

under a rabbit coat. If we'd had regression therapy,
which we didn't because we didn't have time
to be depressed, we wouldn't have been Cleopatra

or an alchemist. No, we'd stretch back through time,
a line of getters-on-with-it and though we're short
on artists and activists, there is the one who stabbed

her husband with the sewing scissors and got shipped
to the back of beyond, one who fled to Cornwall
on account of Daphne Du Maurier and trouble with taxes

and even fearful Enid once went for Alfred's throat
with the edge of a white-hot frying pan, because,
because, she just couldn't be doing with it any more.

Kathy Pimlott

First published in *Under the Radar*, 2018

her defence

I did the thing with pens a
typewriter letters of
complaint cooking tea with
rattles hisses opening
tins packets emptying
bins scrubbing sideways
shelves of cupboards that
rarely see the light scratched
and burned by a knackered
oven I did the things you
said or I thought I
needed to do to keep us
all alive 1am sewing
machine hemming a
dress a perfect seam an
invisible mend clean
up after the dog hoover
the ants from the cereal
cupboard lug the twin
tub out and in three
kids were zipped up inside
me and I let them out one by
one I fed them breakfast
lunch and tea for years
on end hauling the shopping
home I did the things so
what if I open a book mid
afternoon a woman is entitled
to sometimes stop and read

Julia Webb

The Future is Queer

Our house has been vandalised again
they have destroyed our bedroom
our bed while we were away falling more deeply in
impermissible love.
They have violated our oceanic space, reduced it to a lake
only to pollute its lucidity, to poison our goldfish
They have violated our love, called it names, accused it of deceit, inauthenticity.
Because we did not conform; their compulsory heterosexuality pins
them down to their comfortable death beds, yet they rise, from their cold coffins
We laugh non-violently at their violent heteronormativity
They detect the scent of laughter on our lovesucked breaths;
It makes them berserk
They call our survivalist pride, vanity
Our subversive intelligence, snobbery
And our rightful sexuality, abnormality
Our myth-like love, an uncomfortable lie.
They rain and shame, smash and shatter but
We do not utter anything but poetry
they get agitated when we don't look scared
when we gaze back at their violence with our proud faces.

Be patient, my love
The fire of us will escape from
this dungeon and explode their hollow buildings.
Be patient and behold:
Watch us burn.

Golnoosh Nour

Glass Bangles

Auntie Rafia buys me glass bangles, at the Bhori Bazaar
which stretches into the heat haze on both sides
of the Raja Ghazanfar Ali Road —
and she will not let me wear red, *because Debbie,*
these are for married women,

and she says *don't wear too many silver bangles*
they will sound like the clanging of pots and pans
and bangles should slip along the arm
with a sound like a pretty woman's laugh
gentle on the man's ear, and he will know
from the walking music you make how you will
be as a wife.

I have never seen anything so beautiful, these caves of treasure
in the Bhori Bazaar, one after another, stalls high to the ceiling
with colour, and the men who crawl over the stacks of bangles
of glass, smooth as snakes, careful not to break them
to search out the colours, saffron, pink, orange
to pass them down to me, white girl, tourist.

You are a good girl, I can see, not like the others
from the West. You are good girl and wear headscarf,
shlawar chemise; the men on the stalls grin, pass
me stacks of glittering glass bangles, so that I can be beautiful
for one man one day, when I am married.

Auntie loves to haggle, although they are cheap as chips,
we move away, seducing the men with our money
so that the price comes down and down
and go back to the stall where we started and part with the rupees.
And then they are tinkling in paper bags,
like the laugh of a pretty girl wrapped in paper

and we are happy back to the car, but unseen
in the crush, almost like a magic trick it is so swift,
a hand pushes hard up between my legs and hard
and rough against the bone, and another hand
squeezes my breast beneath my rupatta,
my respectful, hide my shape scarf
and pinches and twists hard, and I hear *randi* and *ghora*

and I don't want to ask my lovely Auntie
what those words mean.

Deborah Alma

A Girl Like You

The last place you'd expect
to find yourself trapped in a toilet stall
with a boy you've only just met,
his frame blocking the door,
his eyes gleaming with intent,
and who, you've realised, isn't gay,
is a gay club in Clapham North
where every Saturday the dance floor
teems with men in tight denims
and white T shirts dancing
in a mesh of rainbow light
and always the same mermaid
drag queen smoking at the bar
and while the bass pulses
through the sticky sparkly walls,
he asks again what a pretty girl
like you wants with all these gays,
and your friends, your gentle friends
are clinking shots of goldschlager
in a corner booth, and singing,
you can almost hear them,
it's raining men, hallelujah

Hannah Lowe

Fingered

He put two fingers up
Nicotine tipped
A little prick
Snickering
Balls barely dropped
Hawking up snot to spit cockiness
Chock full of spunk
Tickling mid air
Teasing the pleasure from his waiting mates
Taking the piss, fake masturbating
Grinning a tongue-flicking grin
Ear to ear
Stretched clear to the side
Like knicker elastic, leg lifted leering wide- eyed
His mates hissing

'You lie'
He smeared a skinny pubic-wisped top lip
And sniffed in
Grimacing shit eating smile wiped
Pigeon chested with pride. He sneers
'See it stinks,
She must be rotten inside.
Like something you'd hook Sunday on the side
Of Pennington Flash with your dad
Fish that has long since died
Gutted
Lusty titters
Guffed oohs and phwoars
Become disgusted, twisted, bitter

'Hanging...tramp'
He grabbed his dick
Flicking his wrist,dismissive wanking
Licked his lips
Pretended to gag
The verdict from the lads
'Ewwww.,.you are sick for fingering it'

The girls whispered
'Carol Donnington's a lying bitch
Her tits were the only reason he went with her
He's fit. Have you seen her nails, all bit
They're fake those tips
And he lives in The Limes
He went with that girl kitty
Gets on my wick
I saw them from the bus loads of times
Holding hands like husband and wife
I think he even bought her a ring
Silver, solid not sterling
It's which finger, that's the thing
How you know
Her dad's rich
I'm not being a bitch but a lad like him though
That's the kind he'd go for, the kind he'd get
She's in the top set
Buffed to a shine, filed to points, whitened
Uptight though. She's right stuck up
Toffee nose
She's always got new clothes from the posh shops

The way she smells like...I dunno...Roses
You can tell how well off they are
Better than Carol Donnington by far

His dad drives a sports car. They go abroad. They can afford it.
Cream carpet in the bog, a dulux dog
Gravel on the drive, a brass knocker on the door
I know 'cos me dad laid their floor
They have a bathroom with a separate lav
A lean to. You know like you can have
Carol Partington's mum's a cleaner
I mean
I bet he's been up her
That's why he's keen
As if she's his girlfriend. In her dreams'

In Class 3B Carol Donnington tossed it off
Flicked the market varnished V's
They could believe what they liked
She wouldn't tell tales
Noticed a chip where she'd ate the acrylic
Welled-up, started to skrike
Then thought better of it
Tore it in her teeth then spit
Winced scratching the surface on her lip
Remembered jagged edges
Ripped open petals on flowers on bushes
Torn with thorns
A brass knocker on a door.

Nadia Drews

Bitch

Always just within reach, it is the desk-drawer revolver
or the switch that is flicked when a woman says No
and means No and knows her own mind
and makes herself inconveniently clear;
it is the cocksure roar of boy used to his own way,
one more of the ones we warn each other about,
whose reputations we pass around like classroom
secrets, names itching from girl-hand to woman-hand,
the ones who just love women, who say their wives
really don't mind, the ones who wonder, aloud,
and publicly, what hitch qualifies you to claim
this space for your small fierce self,
the ones who will scrape back their chair, stand up
in the kitsch restaurant, tongue catching on the latch
of that single syllable, the alarmed door he shoulders
open becoming the exit she will depart through.

Jane Commane

Previously published in *#MeToo Anthology*, edited by Deborah Alma and published by Fair Acre Press

every girl knows

i was never more than at fifteen. sick and lovely. see the men
jump out the street to check their shadow. see my high rise
skirt, glass tights, double parked eyeliner, apocryphal name,
smell of monthly embarrassment, suede platforms, scapegoat
thighs, dandruff and blackheads, porn lips, skin lipstick,
yid nose, cheat bra, cheap heart. men were sick cave puppies,
new teeth all over catching sun, rumbling like cars. prepping
the school gates or milling asda whistle wolves clawing for
cookies they would read my tshirt. where you from and
how old do you think and how about a fuckage penetrating
my lopsided ego faith of the worst kind. see the men fall
out the sky to kiss rumour. and my best friend was more.
unequivocally pretty. i would stand next to her and liquify, a
reflect. she get free clothes and steak dinner, pocket money,
jacuzzi hotel room with businessman. manga face curve child
method actor before the abortion. worshipping her slaves, a
confusion. summer camp eves were a tally of kisses. ugly me
with six but only for telling. i slutted as a macguffin, closing
the narrative of last year: fourteen. see the man with kind face
and chub reading storybooks to me and brother. see his hand
placing under dark the wax and wane of his fingers. see my
atomic. see my roadkill. see my throb tick sunburn aerobic
vomit soft breezing through the house wave like a giant whale i
am in the throat of crest of all downhill best days of your life
enjoy it and stop crying look it's top of the pops and kat slater.
i was never more than when i was nothing. i was never i never
did all shhhh and no. i was a pen from melting. objectivity
teething on gobstopper lust i couldn't give away but i gave it.
wet every day like a spaniel's nose. catching flies on the
nightbus, pedalo lake, tube purgatory, blockbusters, park
bench, trocadero, mcdonald's, bridge belly, cherry tree,
corner shop, rope swing, climbing frame all ironic joy but
only wanted or worthless, i and the rest colouring ourselves in

sticky paint and promise, chewing chat, boys in their tshirts
and genes bubbling destiny and if love wasn't boy flavour you
just kept quiet love who said anyway who said love no i only.
if your mouth could sing all the animals out of the forest you
would, wouldn't you. we all method actors pumping puny
cocks for oil waiting for the feelz or feeling daytime soapy
drama but never feeling ourselves. watch out i am so hot i
can't even touch me and days and days of this and not one thing
i would go back for, no not one. did you know if you put
enough posters on your wall you don't need to think, did you
know masturbation is a food group. i am closing on hungry,
peel my upper lip back baby, see how you roll right in.

Amy Acre

First published in the Verve Poetry Competition Community Anthology: *Closed
Gates or Open Arms*

The Daily Grind
Poems that reflect the hardships and peculiar moments of
happiness to be found in our daily lives

'Creation and Sorrow' by Jane Burn

'It is within the massive walls of factory dust and din
That I must woo my humble muse, her favour still to win...
It is amidst pestiferous oil that I inhale my breath,
'Midst pond'rous shafts revolving round the atmosphere of death.'

—*Ellen Johnston* (1835-1873)

On *Joseph Rayner Stephens* was a poem written by a woman known only as 'E.H.,
a Factory Girl of Stalybridge' in which she documents the extreme inequalities
and lack of opportunity and education for working class women trapped by their
circumstances. It is a poem that hopes for reform. She was sent to work in a factory in
what is now Greater Manchester at the age of eight and keenly felt the many injustices.
'If they had sent us to school, better rhymes we could make.' Her poem
was first published in *The Northern Star* in May, 1839.

'Their children, too, to school must be sent,
Till all kinds of learning and music have learnt;
Their wives must have veils, silk dresses, and cloaks,
And some who support them can't get linsey coats.'

J.B., a Checkout Operator meets Factory Girl, E.H.

I'm trying to picture you, as I mindless drag the clutterations
with my practised hand. E for Emily, Edna, Elizabeth, Ethel,
Enid —H for Hallelujiah? Godknows, my forbear. I don't.

Tatties, tatties, staple of the poor —dontcha think you oughttabe
cutting out the stodge? In a different life. This is comfort, filling
a family up on mash. What did you do, mystery E? Cotton or silk —

were you bound in a servitude of cloth? Lungs trapped with fluff,
ears dinned with shuttle-clack, mouth pinned but mind not silenced.
Nailed to the factory at eight —the rest of your life craving school.

You slept beneath the loom. You will never be unravelled.
Who wanted then the ramblings of the poor? Who wants them still?
Let them on high tell us how there's no divide. Map out our lives.

Keep us away from good jobs —in a postcode lottery, in our place.
Claim for your duck-house, cushions, second home. Stuff us
a craw-full of Royals, fool us into kneeling before your Golden Calves,

forget the food banks, needless deaths. E, you put your anger to the page.
Look at the courage you had in writing that. I wish I could tell you that
we're louder now, that bit prouder of who we are. I'll tug a forelock

if it's on the face of a bonny horse. Bow if I'm rooting a cupboard.
Shake hands as an equal or not shake at all. Curtsey? Kiss my arse.
Ain't nobody shutting my mouth. Beep, beep the beer and bottles

of drink, high as kites on BOGOF Lurpak —get your wages, pay them
straight back in. Hours of Trading still means loss of family, loss
of freedom. Thank you, laws for twentyfourseven greed. People working

nightshift, graveyard, clocking in at dawn to miss their kiddies birthday,
miss the birds. You'd laugh at the poster in the locker room, E —the one
that tells you how to look after your mental health. Laugh, or cry.

We're sad, all the time. We get our holidays paid —don't know we're born.
Did you ever even get as far as the Lakes? Did you get time to gather apples
come autumn-time? Where you lived, were there even trees? Working

with some of the best folk you ever met and all in the same boat.
E, I'm sorry. I didn't realise how deep these years of bitterness have run.
I didn't know I'd be so fucking mad.

Jane Burn

First published on *Celebrating Change*

Driftwood Detroit

A city is being sedated
Jesus Christ where are you now!
Listen, for God's sake, to the almost incidental
silver-tongued debates, polished up by cheap liquored
words, marinated for zero hours in all the habitual permanence of a
hotel room, calling it a

town, calling it a town, for God's sake,
not quite meeting byzantine, undisclosed criteria for
numerous reasons, making metallurgy a cyclical, self-deprecating
struggle in authentic better nature and Sunday best pride, keeping an
infant Hercules, juvenile. God I've tried, I've really tried to contort to hard
and brittle, tarred in

over-sized molten alloy footprints,
watching the core of our Constantine College's
foundations quiver and crack, Jesus Christ, I'm an
inshore seagull flying over the tracks from a driftwood
Detroit and you call me a Fishwife! But this is my voice and this,
this is how I cry

Julie Hogg

A Saturday Night

Beneath the fold down seats, full up, largest size,
London cheap shop, black and white checked laundry bag.
Commonplace; beside it, a Sainsbury's Bag for Life, full up.

Man drinks Archers and Lemonade from a can.
Is that a man's drink? His girlfriend asks two tourists.
Unknown territory; blank expressions, language barrier, backs turn.

Made up like she doesn't have a mirror, she winks at me,
beyond youth but youthful, chasing something the night never brings.
She asks me the same thing as I drink Gin and Tonic from a can.
It's a Saturday night?

Uncomfortably familiar cheersing, swigging, laughing,
they know I know, I know they know.

Pale faced rough red patches,
perhaps younger than he looks, eyes of glass, he asks
What percentage?
5%
6.4! You wouldn't think that would ya!

Appropriate communal laughing, tube slowing, they collect the
black and white checked laundry bag and Sainsbury's Bag for Life.
Alight at Elephant.

Southbound time travelling
along the deepest, Victorian route beneath the city
to binge drink with my powdered past.

A cocktail of gin and nerves, topped up with
do you remembers and back in the days
and recognizable changed faces and banging tunes

supplied by swapping smartphones, creates a chemical reaction.

Syncing hearts
accumulate in the kitchen where time is non-existent.
The sink is full of ice and limes crowd the fruit bowl.

Tomorrow's presence is felt.
It can't be getting light?
She flirts her cool, crisp skies through the Venetian blinds,
someone pulls them tighter, but they are fully shut.
The sink is half full of water and discarded squeezed limes decorate the
worktop.

Smartphones unplugged, Ubers confirmed, goodbyes given,
I stay on the sofa, eyes closed awake remembering imagining
listening to people move about in the flat upstairs.

A window opens, TV switched on, monotone male voice of breakfast news
interrupted by commentary of yesterday's football interrupted by,
D'ya wanna cuppa tea? interrupted by... interrupted by...

Becky Bone

All change

Based on a handwritten notebook of recipes from Dorothy Eliza Barnes, (Dot), my grandmother, a shepherd's wife, who had worked as an Edwardian cook.

In schoolgirl hand and blackest black
you scratched down with your steel nib
Puzzle Pudding, Feather Cake,
in neat fast script, no time to think.
Now sky-blue strays into the mix,
light as fire through kindling sticks.
Pencil races. *Elderberry.*
Then biro shakes. No more splashed ink.

B.P. was baking powder. Why?
Did slick self-raising come too late?
Nor did you have penicillin,
Pethidine, or the Welfare State.
Cake with dried egg. You barely paused,
queued, improvised, cooked through two wars.
Slow oven. By my birth, you could
swap coal for cooker, need not wait.

Still you kept adding recipes,
lighter, not heavy, blue, not black.
From *Woman's Own* came Chocolate Cake.
The '60s cooled upon your rack.
With sister, daughter dead, you made
fine curds, great pies, long table laid.
Why did you never show me this?
Beat four eggs well. Do not look back.

Alison Brackenbury

'All Change' was published in *Aunt Margaret's Pudding* (HappenStance Press, 2018). It was broadcast in 2018 in a Radio 4 feature called 'What Sweetness Touched Your Tongue?'

High Fidelity

It is the end of the shift when my hair falls loose:
a single strand of me catches in the sticky tape;
that pin-prick-tug on scalp as I lean forward
to nestle speakers into polystyrene.

I used to wonder what music, what
voices, would make those dark bowls
flex behind their stretched brown cloth.
What type of silences they'd cup.

Already the open box is juddering away
down the black tongue of belt,
smuggling that thread of me away.
My hands hang, heavy as sacks of rice.

I imagined music like large-drop rain;
like feet gliding through paddy field mud;
speech like butterflies in the high bamboo;
news sturdy as headlights.

Zhang Bao slaps on her A1 label;
the metal arms slam the box
shut; the roller parcel-tapes it tight;
and a whisper of me is stowaway.

What remains of me here just hears the dirge
of the rent, the moaning chant of when the train fare
can be scrimped — to return to Qiang who is now three
and has no memory of my voice.

Connection

He is the music buff, I am simply eager
for the polystyrene — perfect drainage
in our biggest plant pots — so snatch
at the nestled speakers. He is steadier;

unpacks the hi-fi ponderously, ticks off
each item on the *How To Assemble* leaflet.
It is because he slows me down
that I find her. Caught in the sellotape.

We are both bent and white now, but she
is jet black, lustrous, long. I hold her
to the morning light spreading through
the mimosa. Is she in Korea or Taiwan,

Hanoi or Beijing; sweat-shop or gleaming factory?
Held to my centre parting, her length drops
to my nipple. Did her nape knot come undone?
Did she feel the tug as the sellotape trapped her,

carried her to another continent?
I hold her limp across both my palms,
show her to him. We both look East.

Char March

First published in *Full Stops in Winter Branches* (Valley Press, 2018)

Dead Pigeons

One wing slanted, the rest of it smeared,
across the pavement in feathered purple violence.
I felt the vomit rise in my throat.
Ew, I said, *look at that.*

Although I don't know why I wanted you to notice such a catastrophe.
I suppose we all need a witness for what we see.
You glanced at it and laughed.
Imagine it's the bodies of your enemies.

My enemies: would I wish their envious, cheating flesh splattered
and so diminished? What once flew on the engine
of abusing me, grounded, gutted, finished,
rotting to pestilence, trampled and ignored, suddenly unlucky.

No. My enemies, I don't wish you were that dead pigeon,
for somehow, that bird is also splendid in its position,
noble in its submission, in its final splayed admission
that this is the place where all suffering ends.

No, my enemies. I wish you worse than that.
I wish you realism. I wish you holes in your shoes,
pennies slipping through your pockets. I wish you struggle,
I wish you this grey pavement on this brown afternoon.

Julia Bell

You can't have weeping in a poem

Sometimes on a Friday I work late,
padding the corridor like a forgotten queen,
the classrooms ragged and empty,
my filthy kingdom laid to waste.
How beautiful, at the photocopier,
to feel us breathe in sync,
worksheets placed cruciform,
a movement so small
the fancy lights go out,
and suddenly the sky, knitted pink.

Sometime when I leave work
late on a Friday night —
the school a hollow behind me,
birdsong echoing at the moon —
my car looks so small
in the streetlight's glare
it makes me think of radar —
those tiny blips that crawl through space,
or lichen, faint and luminous,
circling stone —
and I'm too tired,
too tired to cry.

Catherine Ayres

Free for All

i.m Doll Warner

Before she turned ten they called her
Little Mother. The oldest of eleven siblings,
she knew about ailments — how to attach
string tight to a doorknob and extract a tooth.
She could tempt a TB victim with broth and starve
a fever. She knew diphtheria meant death,
that few people had money for medicine,
or a midwife. She'd race to a stranger's house and boil
water, prepare rags and, often in the dark hours,
persuade a doctor to help for free. For years
she witnessed birth and rigor mortis, saved pennies
to put on dead children's lids. If she was still alive she'd hunt
down her prayer book, find God and scream to Bevan:
Quick! Someone! Save the Nation's Health.

Sally Flint

Home
Poems about migration, displacement, exile and belonging

Image by Imtiaz Dharker

'Exile in its disruptiveness resembles a rebirth for the woman. The pain of breaking out of a cultural cocoon brings with it the possibility of an expanded universe and a freer, more independent self'

—Mahnaz Afkhami.

'O exiles of the mountain of oblivion!
O the jewels of your names, slumbering in the mire of silence
O your obliterated memories, your light blue memories
In the silty mind of a wave in of the sea of forgetting
Where is the clear, flowing stream of your thoughts?
Which thieving hand plundered the pure golden statue of your dreams?'

—Nadia Anjuman, translated by Zuzanna Olszewska and Belgheis Alavi.

My outfit is outlandish as Frances Cornford's poem about a lady in gloves makes me realise that I have feelings for a woman for the first time

I made her a ten-fingered treasure of creamy vintage gloves.
Their softness elevates my shovel bones —if not doves, at least my fists
become a pigeon's common, bloated breast. I am a noir railway farewell,

smoke on the flinty blade of much-spun tracks. I wear them
so she will not see such soiled and work-cracked hands. So I can swank
like I'm something to the station, fabric flamed, underskirt whispering.

Under here I have a tree. A crown of leaves at the cusp of two trunks.
A net to keep the fruit. Five tiers of tulle, sparking. All this
so I can sit my fat in second class, thinking fuck *you*, Frances. You

and your assumptions. There are no ladies, larging it in the fields —
just seed and sheep, horse and copse, hedge and hog, cow and cold
and my indelicacy, studded with magpie brooches, feet primly tucked.

What am I missing? It's true that I wonder if I am loved. I wish I could
peel back the years. I am too old for confusion, yet I muse upon
her thumbs. I follow goslings along the river path, cannot take

them home no matter how the breeze saddens upon on their necks.
It's not my fault they're cold. I let them be, don't want to meet her
livid with the guilt of stolen geese. I see her length flick its whipcord

against the sky. I noise the air, bad as the splash between bow and staith —
should have brought the oppression of my feral days, been subtle
instead of damming the cobbles with garrulous weight. I saw her nape,

her figments of knucklebone, hair. As dusk swapped its dilute for dark,
I snooped the iridescent windows of the dignified rich —peepholes
of taste, floor to ceiling bookshelves, polished tables balmed

by supple lamps. I could stake myself to their lawns, scare the bats
from their primped Box. I could ask but breath never did me no good.
I walked from the room and I could not tell if her eyes had burned

a butterfly on my back. I ran and my heels broke the soul of the stones.
I carry nothing home upon my mouth but the stain of my cold skin.
My heart is the handle that one man will grasp. He'll haul me back,

dump me upon the bed. Unpack with the irritation of laundry day, maul
through the filth of familiar things. Tomorrow, I will crouch, knees
apart in the soil. Against the delphiniums, I will smell my pungent self.

The garden is where I curb or nurture bloom, where I waste my tenderness.
It's rare that I make such journeys. As I bind the gloves in a ball I think
next time, I'll just wear jeans. I love that you are so tall.

Jane Burn

Mi novia se va hoy para Cancún

Mi novia se va hoy para Cancún.
Tiene miedo de que no nos veamos más.
No nos veremos más, estoy segura.
A los tres días de haber llegado un policía corrupto la llevará a la frontera.
Por el camino verá flores y lagartos del desierto.
Será una experiencia espectacular.
Las manos del policía se llevarán
a su casa ochocientos dólares.
Mi novia empezó a comerse una guayaba y un diente se le cayó.
Específicamente la muela que está al lado del colmillo.
Da la impresión de que tiene una piedra ahí.
Está nerviosa por el diente y yo estoy nerviosa
por la frontera.

Los dientes y las fronteras ponen los nervios de punta.

My girlfriend leaves for Cancún today

My girlfriend leaves for Cancún today.
She's scared we won't see each other again.
We won't see each other again, I'm certain.
Within three days of getting there
a crooked cop will take her to the border.
Along the way she will see desert flowers and lizards.
It will be a spectacular experience
                        and the pocket of the cop
will go home with eight hundred dollars in it.
My girlfriend started eating a guava and a tooth fell out.
Specifically, it was the molar that sits next to the canine.
Now she looks like she has a stone where the tooth was.
My girlfriend is worried about the tooth and I am worried
about the border.

Teeth and borders put us on edge.

Legna Rodríguez Iglesias
Translated by *Abigail Parry* and *Serafina Vick*

Packing Two Gold Necklaces

When there is talk of warriors
rarely do they mention the keepers of secrets
or how whole cities have been moved
under the cloak of night
what tiresome work it is
to carry lineage

    which is to hold
your great grandmother and great grandchild
in one hand
and a tasbeeh in the other
you say inshaAllah, God will free us
and prepare for the unknown
often, water
        often, death

When there is talk of warriors
the bustle of kitchens is omitted,
but recipes are strategically altered
in new weather
on new lands

isn't a sword just a knife
that has been repurposed?
Which is to say you have made do

behind the curtains of sons
and into the long memories of your daughters
whose minds are a maze of language
that cannot translate
your name

Nobody will speak of what you left behind
to carry us forward,
least of all yourself

instead:
Allahu aclam /
         God knows best

Hibaq Osman

The bowl

As if she'd been riding side saddle and her body could not quite shake the ridiculous posture now she was back at home, she leant on the right-hand arm of the high-backed chair. Each day is a slow drag to the butcher's, the baker's; those candlestick takers running up back lanes in the dead of night, snuffing out flames with persistent fingers; *we can see you, we can hear you* they snide, as they insinuate themselves between coalhouse and back gate. She remembers the panic on the radio, the rush to the registrar; no one told her about the bargains she'd have to make, the blind eyes she'd have to fake, wincing as she adjusts the dial. How she considers the stain blooming across the cornice as he seethes away, night after night, on top of her. There were times when she flew out of the door and across the city, past the river to where no one else would ever have to squat over a bowl of bleach on the scullery floor. What sort of man brings that home, what sort of man stays after that? The shame of it all falling across the front of the house like the shadow from the barrage. At least she had the children first, because they wouldn't happen now. Not after this. She wipes the bowl, leans it against the taps, he folds the paper on the table and winds his watch.

Lisa Matthews

My grandmothers

were one liners
two word-ers
non speaking parts
tip-toeing trays
into dining rooms
rising before dawn
to riddle ashes
walking home
in too tight boots
on high days
and holidays
bleeding into rags
in secret closets.
My grandmothers
were stitchers
daisy chain and purl
they were
'only women's work'
unwritten poems
stories told
as mere gossip.
They were young once
blushy and bosomy
discovered and undone.
My grandmothers
brewed bitter remedies
read headlines
and heartiness
remembered a time
before bunions
and arthritic handshakes
left recipes instead of diaries
went to their graves

with gold rings
still gleaming
in soft ear lobes
their secrets bagged
in white cotton shrouds.

Pauline Sewards

Moss Side Public Laundry 1979

Childless, I come with a rucksack,
no Silver Cross to steer topple-high
like those bare-legged women in check coats
and bulging shoes who load and unload
ropes of wet sheets, wring them out
to rams' horns while heat-slap of steam
dries to tinsel in our hair, frizzles our lips
gritty with Daz's sherbert dab and the mangle
wide as a room-size remnant
never stops groaning: *one slip and you're done for...*

in the boom and echo of it all their calls swoop
up Cross-your-Hearts, Man. City socks,
crimplene pinks and rayon underskirts, as
Maggie Maggie Maggie Out Out Out! blasts
from across the park, whole streets
get knocked out like teeth,
in a back alley, early, a man
jumped me, shocked as I was
by the words I didn't know I could yell
but which I try out now to make them laugh, these women
who scrub blood and beer and come
with red brick soap, quick-starch a party dress
while dryers flop and roar, before their kids fly out from school
flock outside for a smoke's sweet rest
from the future bearing down,
four walls and one man.

Pippa Little

Disappeared

That look I recognise. The women's faces
have been cut away by scalpels of light,
pared so hard the person has disappeared.

White forehead, white cheekbones, black holes
where the eyes once were. They hold up the photographs
of husband, brother, son, the other disappeared.

They have turned the faces outward for everyone to see,
in case someone witnessed the nudge on the street
or saw them taken aside, or heard the knock on the door,

in case there is Information.
If they are speaking at all they are saying a name,
but all speech is lost in the wailing of sirens.

They hold up the faces of family men
who have been devoured on the usual road home
or swallowed whole by the exit door

and the photograph is a shield the women wear
over the heart, all the brightness turned outward
to where no-one is looking, really, no-one

is watching; towards a reason that may not be there,
really, a world that might as well have disappeared.

Imtiaz Dharker
First published in *Over the Moon* (Bloodaxe, 2014)

Girl Golem

The night they blew life into me, I clung
bat-like to the womb-wall. A girl golem,
a late bonus, before its final egg dropped.
I divided, multiplied, my hand-buds bloomed,
tail vanished up its own coccyx, the lub-dub
of my existence bigger than my nascent head.

I was made as a keep-watch,
in case new nasties tried to take us away.
The family called me *chutchkele*, their little *cnadle*,
said I helped to make up for lost numbers –
as if I could compensate for millions.

With my x-ray eyes, I saw I was trapped
in a home for the deaf and blind, watched them
blunder into each other's craziness. My task,
to hold up their world, be their assimilation ticket,
find a nice boy and mazel tov – grandchildren!

But I was a hotchpotch golem, a *schmutter* garment
that would never fit, trying to find answers
without a handbook. When I turned eighteen,
I walked away, went in search of my own kind,
tore their god from my mouth.

Rachael Clyne
From *Girl Golem* (4Word Press)

* Golem — a mythical man made of clay & Kabbalistic spells to protect the Jews
from persecution.

Inside / Outside
Poems that focus on issues of "health", physical and mental

Image by Jane Burn

'Caring for myself is not self-indulgence. It is self-preservation, and that is an act of political warfare.

—*Audre Lorde*

'Has anyone spoken to me today? A product of fears and phobias.
Who transcends immortality by killing herself before remembering
how much she loved the earth this life. To distance myself
From hatred I have nothing to say to inquisitorial people...'

—*Anna Mendelssohn*

While I waited for the tablets to kick in

no silence, baby/a sure attack/ imagine a desire to repent/
love is quite spare/ointment over and over/out, cohesive earmark/
divine dissent/plateau of another antique philosophy/
common sombre track/a person with loose bowels/encased in austerity/
dear memory/quarter marks on my new floor/it's quite a colourful place,
no comparison/love comes included/my dolorous and dull pupil/
tantalizing bandit, to you I venture/private and docile/
I will desire an avenue of flowers/a language of polite imagination/
some can, some cannot/you are my dear corpse/you nourish me
I am partial to you/no banquets or convivial silences/
no decades consigned to others/ecstasy does not quantify time passing/
we will not depart this private episode/no longer the last messy paragraph
of us/but a quiet, temperate day

Jane Burn

First published on *Algebra of Owls*

NOT a dissertation on how shit your life is

(For everyone who has filled one of those form)

Please fill in the following in blue or black ink, red lipstick, mauve crayon, pink glitter or don't.

Question 1)
Please write down the address of the place you felt the safest, the furthest from harm,
where you can breath, where you can be yourself, use your imagination if needs be, if your imagination has broken, or become stained by life, this is not your fault, you can use mine, mine wants you to be happy

Question 2)
How would you like to be contacted?
Please tick all that apply.
With respect
with due care and attention to your individual circumstances,
softly
gently
with acessible, concise words
in a way you understand
without a brown letter
with warning
what font do you prefer,
we're sorry

Question 3)
Are you
a) awesome
b) awesome wonky
c) wonky with strains of awesomeness

Question 4)
What was good about today?

Question 5)
What 5 things should we not presume about you?

Question 6)
Please draw your grandmother's smile in the box below

Question 7)
What sweets did you like as a child?

Question 8)
What are 5 things you can do.

Question 9)
Who has loved you.

Question 10)
What have you overcome? In the least patronising way —
well done, it's not always easy.

Question 11) How would the world be different if you
were in charge?

Jackie Hagan

Functioning

I am having trouble stringing sentences together
she said

I am having trouble breathing
I am feeling very sad
she said

I am angry all the time, I am sad
she said

as she ate a forkful of mushroom and tomato spaghetti

I am due to see the doctor
she said

as she scooped up some mozzarella

Can the doctor cure me?
she said

as she sipped on a Diet Coke

I am afraid of solipsism
she said

as she popped an olive into her mouth

Can they cure that?
she said

Her dad said
Yes

Nicki Heinen

Low pressure

Calm. That means I would never chase you. This idea comes quietly
in commotion, when the midnight wind fires rockets, grazing our sides.

It's true, I once ran along the tyre tracks of departing cars: wide alert
while the storm tossed cabers, my habit was to race, thump on windows

gasping, rain in my eyes, *Why are you leaving me?* How, then, did you and I
turn love into a present participle, so that now we lie in the arms of night,

and I hear you breathe the same equable breaths you'd take with just the
spilling gutter for company? I cannot sleep, and in the branch-torn morning

will not recall my words' form. A thought about a dark fly landing on the lamp.
Maybe how it would not, in the past, have sat there long enough for scrutiny.

But listen while you sleep, love. Hear me renounce those reckless vows,
the hook I could never reach. I have entered a new life. Dug in. Here.

In peace or turbulence, I am immune to the needle's swing. I mean it.
You and I will hang our thoughts, each in our own place. And we will meet.

Sarah Wedderburn

Reality box

The box can take it all:
look. The future deaths of my children.

There is nothing it turns away:
My children's terrible deaths,
The train with only black through its window.

The box is indiscriminate,
It maitre d's for the deaths,
It signals, darkly, for the train in the dark.
It punches the plane through the sky, downwards.

You have to give the box credit, you do.
Nothing is turned away;
It swallows the plane whole —
it is quite magical that the box can do this
— the plane that now sits noiseless, smashed and unseen in the dark.

Inside the box, I am held down in the ground,
It keeps me parched and frantic in the tunnel.
It attacks my husband on the ordinary street.
Everything is muffled: my exploding heart,
my exploding head.
The box has it all:
My husband and the street,
My husband's hidden body, never there, always there.
The exploded world waiting in the box.

Natalie Shaw

My Girlfriend Did Not Believe in Ghosts

though her sister wore trainers in bed
so she could run quickly
though they kept her awake for days
though they were there
though they walked heavily through our rooms
and made the floor shake
though we were under attack
though there was a darkness
and the door was pulled from its hinges
though nothing moved
though they banged on the walls by our bed
and made her sick
though the priest came
though he could not cast out my spirit
though he tried
though my mother woke each night
who art in heaven
though there was whispering
though my brother saw lights in the dark
though I woke to a man in my room
though my father saw me through the window
though I was not there
though I looked him in the eye
and walked away
though I lived with them all of my life
though I knew myself
though I was honest
though strangers asked who was upstairs
though no-one was
though I lived through the end of times
and I found feathers
though there was someone in the house
it was not us

though no-one touched me
though it would not leave me alone

Clare Shaw

Our Lady of Malaise

Forgive my knots and maladies,
the litany of bad days.
And praise the sheepdog mind
that twitches awake
at two a.m. to round up
stray words into a pen.
Bless the woman who understands
the cascade of events,
the language of pain:
every knife attack,
shark bite
and crashing wave.
Give thanks for the one
who understands the canyon
of fatigue, its sheer drop
and tumbling rocks.
And bless the brain
like a phone that can't hold its charge.
The calls that can't be made.
And when another winter
of the soul brings me again
to the shrine at Tether's End,
I know I am not alone
for thou art with me, there,
waiting at the window
in a dirty nightshirt, so tired
you could cry, haloed
in a streetlamp's gold,
watching over the lost women
struggling home through the snow,
and those who walk in circles below.

Joanne Key

Bird-Watching

Counted fifteen dead birds on the lawn this morning waiting for the maggots to come.
I tried to see what the other writers evidently saw beyond the extinction hysterias and
      manifestos
But, it wasn't birds —there was nothing for me, no demiurge. My universe does not want
      to meet yours;
And whilst A listers fly great distances to attend air travel protests, I ask myself
What a bird's eye view of myself could mean whilst I'm buried or bored.

Don't you remember that summer when my broken skin would reflect all light and sound
      from the pounding?
The young have taken to bird-watching and anal sex. The state of Grace has gone
      unreplicated.
My stepfather accused me of destroying his marriage because I gave him a Ouija board
On his fifty-first birthday. I was taking so much acid at the time. Of course,
Who knows what supernatural things happen to us without our knowing.

From the garden pool I step on a frog, onto a needle, into a very deep sleep.
I sleep hard with the head of a bird, the coma is wild, I read about twenty-one years later
I died. I was a worm afraid of all things bird-related, which would be entirely obvious
      should you ever
Be that low in the ground. The Doctor told me he'd seen it too and asked me what I found
      —Sir,
The soil was terribly claggy and neutral and the subsequent flight into the arms of a man

I had no desire to love was just as bad. I broke up with him over the phone. I became
      extremely good
At writing. A period of incarceration as a psychotic post-coma patient led me to detain
      my body
With a complement of drugs. My friends were imagined. There were such tales reported
      of the birds
Who watched me squirm against the hands of physicians. They recorded all the swear
      words I said.
I whirred my index finger round in the air as though I knew what I was doing, to
      frighten them.

So now you're here what will you do with it? Your sight. Your lack of intuit. I always knew
There was something in me birds admired. The way they crashed into my windows on sight.
The way they nested in my bedclothes, nourished on bed-bugs, danced on my fingertips.
My stepdad said I was allergic. Anaphylactic shock once killed me, I laid there whilst he
        prophesied,
'She's going to die.' It interested me to have this subjective viewpoint of the way I was
        objectified.

Now I do remember all the times I've been held down, pinned. But to even talk
Takes more cells than I can use these days. Yes, do stay in the city with your little sun-hats
        and Jesus,
He loves you of course, far more than anyone else. I was always sensitive to my family's
        comedy
Depictions of me saving starlings and sparrows from certain death, spinning around with
        their
Delicate bodies in my open palms, spinning until they'd invariably fall out and die on the
        roadside.

I made epic contraptions to house spiders in, believing it better for them. Their skeletons
        seemed to
Vanish quite soon into a feint brown dust. I thought you knew what was best when you
Had me committed. I missed stealing ice lollies from the old man's sweet shop on Bank
        Holidays,
And having skin fall off in chunks from my face. It was the purgatory I deserved; I suppose.
It was easier existing in that windowless place. I just wish that you'd called.

Melissa Lee-Houghton

This Poem has a Title

This poem must take medication in order to be read
at any future event. It has been found that this poem
has an unfair natural advantage which makes it stand
out at festivals and open mic spots, and streak ahead
of its competitors. In order for the competition not to
feel demoralised, this poem must take aural contraceptives
to suppress its innate ability to propagate and inspire
other poems to try as hard as this poem. This poem
must be sterilised, and wake up lethargic and drugged,
so it becomes a non-starter and will be stripped of its title.
This poem has too many phonemes which must significantly
be reduced to sub-haiku levels. However, if this poem
refuses to subscribe to its prescription, it may be allowed
to focus on becoming a long poem of 5,000 lines
where new rules regarding the phoneme levels do not
apply. It is accepted that this ruling is discriminatory,
but is necessary, reasonable and proportionate
to ensure fair competition for all poems that are just not
as good as this poem. Any argument that this poem
should be celebrated, not regulated, will be ignored.
The future of this poem has been brought to you by
a panel despite its serious concerns about this poem
having to take frequent medication, absence of evidence
and potential harmful side-effects of phoneme treatment.
This poem has promised to fight. This poem will be heard.

Lisa Kelly

The Last Time I Got Hysterical in The Middle Of The Night

Actually, it started about an hour ago.
Or at least, I reached hysteria about then.
So I went and woke him up, as I often do,
and he came and sat with me while I vented.
He reminds me that I will feel better in the
morning, that it's a waking nightmare,
nothing to worry about, perfectly natural,
just part of the process. Last week I threw
the remote at him, to stop some of his
hysteria perhaps (he never does it in the night),
or in fury and frustration at his memory
problem, his "I need to be looked after"
raising its childish wail again. But I can't
remember what it was on that particular
occasion, and nor can he. I nearly broke
the remote, though, another irritation
to add to the daily pile. Perhaps it was
because of that calm and rational voice,
droning on in the night, when sanity
feels like a straitjacket, and all my fears
are mountains not to be conquered or crossed.
Now he's gone back to sleep – he can
always sleep – and I've not to let the
monsters off their chains again, I've got to
not cross bridges, not allow my imagination
free range, I've got to bear the unbearable,
unthink the unthinkable. I can feel the fear
and rage jerking and pulling, and the
anxiety about how I will cope revving up
to a full-blown fit of the Violet Elizabeths,
and it's four o'clock now and I've got
to get up in the morning and raise a smile.

Rosemary McLeish

Last Chance for this Earth
Poems relating to our precarious environment

'Lady with Honey Hair and a Crown of Bees' by Jane Burn

'Wherever women acted against ecological destruction or/and the threat of atomic annihilation, they immediately became aware of the connection between patriarchal violence against women, other people and nature, and that: In defying this patriarchy we are loyal to future generations and to life and this planet itself.'

—*Maria Mies*

'Ecofeminism is about connectedness and wholeness of theory and practice. It asserts the special strength and integrity of every living thing. For us the snail darter is to be considered side by side with a community's need for water, the porpoise side by side with appetite for tuna [...] We are a woman-identified movement and we believe we have a special work to do in these imperilled times. We see the devastation of the earth and her beings by the corporate warriors, and the threat of nuclear annihilation by the military warriors, as feminist concerns. It is the masculinist mentality which would deny us our right to our own bodies and our own sexuality, and which depends on multiple systems of dominance and state power to have its way.'

—*Ynestra King*

From the margins

By Cathy Dreyer

There are many truths told about the importance of women writing the planet in poetry. And there are many lies.

The biggest lie is that women have a special connection with the planet because we are women. This lie says that because women and our wounded planet share the capacity to create and sustain life, to mother, that we share a sympathetic bond no other gender can understand. This is an obvious lie, and part of an exclusionary politics that Fran Lock disavows in the Introduction to this anthology. Many women do not or cannot have children, and the planet can be, often is, and has always been, deadly for many people.

Ideas about both the planet and women as inherently nurturing are surely cultural ideas and, when they erase other facets of what it means to be a woman, or a planet, they are potentially dangerous. If, for example, we say that our reproductive biology makes us more likely to feel concern for the future, to feel, even, a sense of moral obligation to protect the environment for the sake of any children we might have we may suddenly find that our imperiled right not to be mothers, our right to terminate pregnancies, is further undermined. What are embryos if not, potentially, future generations?

As the climate emergency grows ever more urgent, it becomes harder and harder to warn that the logic of environmental concern can be difficult for women in other ways, especially since climactic disasters tend to threaten women disproportionately. Here, in the developed West, many of us are not yet scared, or not scared enough. We are not scared enough to give up our washing machines, our fridges, or the contraceptive pill. These are all pollutants, yet they have all also been fundamental to women's liberation.

As Fran Lock argues in the essay 'This Land is Our Land', we cannot afford to be romantic about the land. Here, I argue that the same goes for the planet. The poetry I want to read emerges from shared concerns and experiences rather than fantasies about essentialist Gaia-feminism. Globally, women's lives vary. Motherhood remains, of course, an experience many women share. There are other experiences we are likely to share. Despite some gains, we are still far more likely to be poor than men, earning almost half as much as they do[1].

---

[1] *The Global Gender Gap Report*, World Economic Forum, 2016

We own less than five per cent of guns globally[2]. Our poverty and restricted choice is multiplied if we are women of colour, or disabled women, or LGBT women. We are, in short, less likely to be among the powerful and free within patriarchal capitalism, a global trading system sustained by military might.

Given the difficult reality of lives at the sharp end of this data, it seems crass to suggest that there is anything positive to be said about being poor and oppressed. It does mean, however, that as a group we have less to lose from systemic change. We can see ourselves as less wedded to things as they are and more open to transformation.

With TV ads in rhyming stanzas and many laureates being women, it's fair to say that poetry, and women's poetry in particular, is going through a period of relative popularity. In the main, however, patriarchal capitalism is not very interested in poetry. Unlike film, pop, and even fine art, poetry is not considered worth co-opting. Glamorous red-carpet parties are vanishingly rare in poetry. And it is poetry's persistently neglected hair and over-stretched knicker elastics, its *eau de unshaved armpit*, which open the door for poems about the planet to be a vital resource. Women, disproportionately living in poverty and without freedom, are over-qualified in Cinderella skills. Many of us perhaps find the often marginalized space of poetry rather familiar and are pleased with the opportunity to examine and re-form oppressive cultural ideas with little interference from the worlds of money and power.

The poems that follow this essay determinedly slough off the deadly romance of women's 'special' communion with the planet and offer hope for a transformed future. Jane Burn's powerful 'I gave/my shame/to water/ it told me/nothing about/myself' is embedded in the grit and dailiness of living ('/feral squat to piss on roots/'), using form to suggest, simultaneously, the density of embodied experience and the fragility of the stories we tell about it. Her text dances brilliantly and impossibly on the edge of coherence. Angela Topping's 'Stone Dress' deftly surprises us with unmisty-eyed hope and a call, perhaps, for us to transform our understanding of our resilience even as it is anchored in the experience of difficulty. By contrast, Sarah Doyle reminds us, in 'Night Shifts in the Nature Factory' of what is at stake and why the truth about the climate emergency is the truth which should scare and anger us into telling it more than any other.

---

[2] Data is difficult to find. But a 2014 report by the Small Arms Survey found that in nine countries for which data is available women owned 4% of guns in civilian hands and combat troops in the world's armed forces remain overwhelmingly male, only about 20 countries accepting women in these roles.

I gave/my shame/to water/it told me/nothing about/myself

a kill of un-done bones/heron's moveless stain/quiet worlds of moss/tilt
of riverbank/kingdom of frogs/vein of silver fish/weak baste of sun's eye/
remember the/language of my mother's hands/feral squat to piss on
roots/ oh I wanted/thin rake of dusk/I saw a woman/wear a crown of dull
sky/ here is a gift of throats/the water wears a skin of ghosts/you will not/
meet/the craving of cold palms/oh I saw a woman/reflections of trees/
are a desire of knives/fecund splay of spawn/wound of coming night/
I hear/your breath/your heart/a claim of fallen moons/a trick of wet

Jane Burn

Waste Disposal

Where is the will, imagination, thought, instinct,
self-imposition that gets you to a better place,
a higher plain? What have onlooker's seen
but savage and stupid, binge-like broken instincts,
toxins with no quick-fix antidote, freak-show-style contestants

cooped up in grim-rimmed chicken grids for homes,
their bladed cages promising sharper, steelier freedoms
beyond and stab at the sleekest glint of self-improvement.
Inevitability is government policy at its most austere, MPs
playing bow and arrow from the glistening turrets of Shitehall.

Social mobility is segregating buses and schoolrooms
and city centres; it's being granted permission to breathe,
to smell the weed-wrangled breath of your neighbour
on the other side of the wall: his rising damp, your rising damp:
in the soup with asthmatic, nicotine-hungry kids
who are kicked in the head before they know
what disadvantaged is.

Clare Saponia

From *The Oranges of Revolution* (Smokestack Books, 2015)

Stone Dress

It took a long time to grow,
this marble studded with fossils.
A difficult dress to wear,
lacking the glamour of silk,
but suited to all weathers.
It made her feel safe, impermeable,
a cave house where none
could touch her.
She wore a stream for a scarf,
tied her hair with brambles,
wove shoes from green nettles.
Stepping out in this array
she was newly bold, unconquerable.

Angela Topping

Night Shifts in the Nature Factory

We make birds here. Crows, ducks, owls,
gulls: feathers glued to papier mâché wings,
legs fashioned with matchsticks. We carve
seeds from plastic, beat metal until it turns
to trees. We cast fossils. We tint skies with
water-colour and stoke the smoke of clouds.
We add salt to vats of sea, and stir. We forge
rats, foxes, cows, wolves, worms — winding
the cogs of their mechanisms tightly, for luck.
We bake summers in a kiln and chill winters
inside a walk-in fridge. We can synthesise
night with the flick of a switch. Close your
eyes, spread out your hands like stars:
and look, we have hammered you a moon.

Sarah Doyle

Highly commended, Ginkgo Prize for Ecopoetry, 2018, and previously published
in the prize anthology

How I Mistook The World For A Cow

It's true I thought the world was a large cow.
I used to drain her bulgy dugs most days.
I blame the world for this. The world allowed
me to believe she was a cow, the way
she'd moo on cue and give me milk to drink
and even when I tethered her too tightly,
she only twitched her tail and let me think
that she rather liked behaving cowishly.
I mean, she never tried to get away –
she never bellowed to be fed or sheltered,
just stood, slow-blinking, at what came her way,
unmoved by belching trucks and cars that pelted
past. Oh well. So, the world is not a cow.
How will I fill my empty stomach now?

Cathy Dreyer

Talking Trees

Rough to touch, I breathe into my warm
fractured skin. Other trees held me
tighter, but I know your lines, bumps and knots

and tonight you say *There is no free will.*
The oddest thing I ever saw carved into a tree
was a stamp that said *made in Bangladesh*

and I didn't like it. I had no buds or saplings
just toes and fingers, and thought I couldn't bare it
all those sleepless nights, I was Rhododendron,

saw a winter inside summer leaves,
the love of green to cling before the blood
of fall. My fir trees died in a shudder

of lightning, all splinter and sap. I suck
it up, pretend it didn't happen, those catastrophes,
turn you into a singing ringing tree, sit on top

in a taffeta dress unfolded from an acorn.
I hold one seed out to you, *take it — keep it safe
for my sake, and we'll meet later at the next clearing.*

I saw things in the trees near that housing office
where we signed on — at Medina Road,
years ago, you tell me, *They cut them down,*

they're not there any more. Then I will go, find
the clearing in a hazel grove, collect winter into fruit
at the water's edge, live in heron's nest,

talk to the oldest tree in Britain, hug it's tough skin,
give it birthday presents, be friends with it, become
its fruit, be dispersed by blackbirds.

Jessica Mookherjee

Held hard and fast

Thickness of earth between my toes
is not enough, and yet too much.
It draws me down, holds my skin
in such a tight embrace, I'm sound,
the ground my inescapable domain.
Some may wish for gills, a way
to breathe in water, insist the sea
could be their home again. Not me.
I want only air in waves that barrel endlessly
to lift me on the tides of warmth that rise
and let me spread once more my loss
of wings, a mattered memory of glide.
Inside my head I'm always airborne, escaping
every failure felt as astronaut, as kite,
as tiny skimming hummingbird in flight.

Denni Turp

Creed
Poems relating to our spirituality

'Our Lady of the Barricades' by Fran Lock

Oh spirits of dead centuries! Reverent, wise,
Brave, active, generous, fraught with all that's blest,
The Soul that nurtured yours within us lies;
We have your longings vast, at times your rest;
And we, as you, — our apathies apart —
Have wants and woes within us — a full heart
Of something vast, unspoken — something wise,
Which through the darkness still sustains our eyes.

—*Mary Smith* (1822-1889)

In name of the Three of Life
In name of the Sacred Three,
In name of all the Secret Ones,
And of the Powers together,

—*Isabella Chisholm* (1865-1882)

Look at me, lingering outside this murdered church

Open your lids, you coal-smut, bitter thing. Undraw the blind
that your plunged doom has set in the lead of your eyes.
Too many years of chimneys, licking their filth on your bricks.
Nobody comes to pluck at your weeds. Look at the pair of us,
our caverns unused. Methodists didn't build for beauty —
face like a mortuary slab, barren grim of harsh white walls,
let me in and I'll sing you some saints. God, for me has not
been enough. If I am to believe, daub me some vivid grief,
gouge this wasted cave with a burning of Sacred Hearts.
I will treat this bare render with my own crude litter of faith.
You were laboured, foundations up by your devout, by the skill
of women and men — they met and worshipped, passed
the plain, small wealth of the humble plate. Against your shell,
I hear the memory of Sunday School, feel the holy flattening
of my arse after hours spent pressed to the hard-wood seat,
colouring between the lines of Gentle Jesus, playing with
the brittle thin of simple, twisted palm. Thus we were made
by a plain religion. I craved the gibber of rosaries, the veils,
the fondant of Communion gowns, the thurible swinging
the fume of dedication up. The wailing visions of Virgin's smalt,
the tabernacle with its myth of Saviour's blood. My prayers
will splatter your emptied crypt with a mess of devotion.
My hymns are huge. I am an exorcism. Am here to spew
my devils at your altar's feet, did not expect to find
the slam and hasp of ailing Gothic doors. I make
what I think is the requisite sign, poking my relic of belly
and tits. An empty cross to show that I already suffered and won.
Open up, you barred and bolted thing.

Jane Burn

Move Along Now

So what was it like to grow up in a cult?

Normal, just normal. Everything's fine,
officer. Everything's fine, social worker.
We can raise our children how we want to.

Stop persecuting us! These are our
walls. This is our loving Family. We eat all
meals together just like anyone (except
that the vegetables talk to us). We believe

school creates an army of mindless drones.
Oh, that's a cigarette burn, not a BGC scar.
No vaccinations here. Doctors are tools

of the corporate brainwashing state.
All the shrinks want is to lock us away.

Blood purifies us. Rage purifies. We had to
imprison her for her own good, nurse. She
agreed to all this before she was born,
magistrate. Our sacred leader told us so.

Oh he's been dead years, but he still talks
to us. Possesses our bodies, just like normal.
Everyone is happy and perfect, journalist.

How dare you all keep calling us a cult.

Maya Horton

Erased

God loves you they said, as they took the rubber to my face, on keyring fobs and photo frames, not a ghostly outline left. I stalk the streets well in this invisible cloak. A rainbow smile left at the gate as they watched me somersaulting down the broad path to destruction years ago. Up it pops again, the last meal, the grandparents, the cousins, the aunts, the uncles, the agreeable smiles, you, little brother, who did not cry in five years as my grief sits behind a hand on the pane. You imagined me racing in the game of life, the million-pound house, raucous laughter and party hats full of opportune jokes and debauchery in the streets. Except I wear muted colours, I've shed the sunshine, emptied the blue skies and sit in the quiet of the night breathing in the wisps of my daughter's hair, listening to the silent voices speaking to me so loud they have shattered all the mirrors, cutting my fingers as I try to piece them back together like a mosaic. It's so simple they state. The fault is mine. Just come back. God will forgive you.

Laura Lawson

St Rose of Lima's Revenge

At a rough-backed hour, wound round with olive
light, the pink-cheeked would-be anchorite
slides past date palms and scarlet
trumpet lilies in the colonial garden, intent
on the far spinney, where wiry trees like acolytes
surround a simple hut her heart always skips to reach.

Holy time, before the porcelain-jowled suitors
(damn them!) begin to queue,
their arms and brows pale-as-the-dough
which Madre leaves in the sideways sun
to rise. Their insect-voices urgent and *'mi-querida'*-ing
as they bend low to moan her name.

Always always she is called back just when
hermano Sun peeks up to play, called back
along the manicured paths, the geometric beds.
Called back from the bosky place, cloaked in *verde*
and all alone with the *Belovedexpected*. Called in
by a maid as 'Señor So-and-So is waiting (and his
father is so *importante*, pretty Rosita)'.

She makes lace, and takes stupendous blooms
to market, to support the house, 'though many in the city
are much worse-off, *Mami'*. Some of those poor she brings
to her room, to rinse and bind till nightfall. Then,
though drooping, keeps vigil, to cultivate that sweet edge
of encounter, and grow —oleander-like— glossy with blessing.

Siesta-time, she flits again —lizards skid
on scalding sand— down to the cool grotto, for an hour
in eucalyptus and blueberry, till, again, some
Rafael or Gregorio in the lobby, and oh, the slippery grasping
insistence when you are so spent and your legs and arms so limp
and the cushions in the parlour so soft and grateful.
Ah, but she'll show them. She plucks two pods as she passes in

at the kitchen door, scores their seams, then draws tart flesh
and virgin seeds across her eyelids, and cheeks,
like a society lady's brightener, and they begin
to smart and swell. 'Ah, my Rosa at last!' her mother turns,
then gasps, at Rosa's eyes dancing and red, the perfect skin
puckering into pustules, fresh chilli juice dripping
at her fingertips. The suitors look, and look away. But then (covertly)
look again.

Geraldine Clarkson

Commended in the 2015 National Poetry Competition, and originally published
by the Poetry Society.

The Red Admiral Butterfly

Sitting there, my stiff sore body, my muscles contracting causing me agonising pain. My mind wanders as I sit looking out of the window, my eyes have no focus so I can't see much other than a blurry mess, looking on as a bystander.

My two younger sisters, one a teacher, the other a nurse, my mother a NHS administrative worker and my father always having a variety of manual jobs. But me, I was a nobody, I just faded into society. I lived within the community but I never felt part of it.

My upbringing has taught me to have a strong work ethic, in my mind I was a worker, but I had nothing to work at. I was the eldest of three children, and my two younger sisters had overtaken me in their lives with their achievements. I have never been jealous of them. Envious, maybe? I wouldn't be human if I didn't feel envious from time to time. I never wanted to mirror their lives, but I wanted to have a life of my own, different but of equal significance and achievement. But there I was trapped in my broken body. I was 30 years of age at the time, contemplating another 30 years like this, like a spare part, surplus, great. The mere thought filled me with dread.

After myself and my family struggled, and fought tooth and nail to enable me to achieve independent living, was this it, really?? ..... A walk into town looking round the shops with no money to buy anything, or no real reason to be there, was this all life had to offer me? I was simply wasting my days away. On one occasion I was so bored that I fell asleep walking around the supermarket.

Life was grim. Soon after, followed a period of darkness. A big black hole of nothingness. A hole so big I felt as if I couldn't escape. I so desperately wanted to experience life. I longed for friends, a partner, the chance of opportunities of any kind.

Growing up I'd always been very close to my grandparents, who'd both passed away some years earlier. I'd missed them greatly. One day during my time of depression, the sun came streaming though the widow, the window that I'd been sat looking out of on many occasions. It was just the brightest light, the warmest most comforting feeling. I continued with my day, and as I left the house to take my dog for her daily walk, the support worker who was working with me at the time said, 'Hannah your buddleia is full of red admiral butterflies, you know what that means, there's people looking down on you.' So I didn't really think much of it. These beautiful butterflies kept appearing day after day. Maybe it was just a coincidence, but I feel that they have been sent by my grandparents, showing that they were with me in spirit.

Within 3 months I began sailing and loved it. Within 6 months of becoming a sailor I'd also collaborated on a project that aimed to give those with disabilities opportunities through music, establishing them as musicians. This adventure is still ongoing. By this time I also had many friends.

To go from having nothing to do, nowhere to go and no one like-minded that I could relate to. From feeling that I had no prospects and my life feeling so empty. I was very soon participating in society, I was playing an active role in the community, was at last being given the opportunity to thrive, to achieve goals, to meet people and build and maintain meaningful relationships.

I've grown wings and flown as a person. My life is bright and colourful, just like the beautiful red admiral butterflies my grandparents have sent to watch over me, and guide me, as a constant reminder that they're never far away. My grandparents spirit lives on through me, they're with me in all that I do, through good times and bad. They're with me during every sailing competition, during every musical composition I create. I am now living my own life, as opposed to being a bystander watching everyone else live theirs. I now live life with a smile, making life a lot easier, making life worth living.

I will finish it with a quote:

The magnificent life of the butterfly closely mirrors the process of spiritual transformation as we each have the possibility to be reborn through going within.

— author unknown.

Hannah Shelmerdine

Outro:
"But you're here, aren't you?"
The place of working-class women in the arts and academia

By Fran Lock

I've written before about how the so-called "triumphs" of working-class representation in the arts... um... really aren't; how, in reality, the rhetorics of "representation" have led to a selectively edited picture of working-class identity across multiple cultural platforms, a situation in which one or two—usually white, usually old, usually male—voices have become icons and ambassadors for a complex network of cultures and experiences. The "representation" paradigm favours tick-box statistics over richly storied subjectivity, and thus works to erase the persons it purports to signify. This is a real hobby-horse for me, but what I haven't written about in nearly as much detail is how this situation disproportionately affects women, or how it feels to be one of those women.

Shit. In a word. And a report from the Social Mobility Commission published earlier this year confirmed what we already knew through years of bitter personal experience: that we continue to earn less and to occupy fewer professional positions than those of privileged backgrounds. The figures are stark. Working-class people in professional jobs earn almost a fifth less than their more privileged colleagues, colleagues who are 80 per cent more likely to make it into a professional job in the first place. Quelle my complete and utter lack of surprise.

We're told that the increasing numbers of students from disadvantaged backgrounds entering university is a signal of unequivocal progress, yet the fact remains that working-class people are more likely to "drop out"— and I *hate* that phrase, by the way, it sounds volitional, as opposed to, say, systemically engineered—before graduating, and that we still face higher levels of unemployment after university, despite overall employment increasing.

Summing up the report's findings, Dame Martina Milburn, chair of the Social Mobility Commission had these grave—but to working-class women, blindingly obvious—words to say: "Being born privileged means you are likely to remain privileged. But being born disadvantaged means you may have to overcome a series of barriers to ensure you and your children are not stuck in the same trap."

She's not wrong. The report also found that women in England with postgraduate degrees still earn less than men with only bachelor's degrees, and that black graduates across all age groups were the lowest paid, and also least likely to find employment in professional or "high skilled" occupations.

Just think about that for a minute. And then imagine *being* a working-class person in one of these jobs, imagine being a woman in one of these jobs, imagine being a black, or culturally "other" woman in one of these jobs: there you are, in this hypothetical thought-experiment universe, attending some stodgy "networking" event, milling about with your middle-class colleagues, when you hear one of them say, quite loudly and quite confidently, that we're now living in a post-class society.

I kid you not, this actually happened. And yes, in the Choose Your Own Adventure Story I console myself with in my head, I also hit him with a lukewarm vegetarian snack-platter. But cathartic as that is, it doesn't help us isolate exactly why and on how many level's he's wrong. So let's take a deep breath and do that instead.

One of the things working-class girls learn to do early on is switch registers. We're much more dexterous than boys at pin-balling back and forth between modes of speech; between restricted and elaborated language codes and the social roles that engender them. Working-class girls will have a school voice, a home voice, and a street corner voice, which gives us a bit of superficial social mobility, but it also condemns us to daily acts of self-induced schizophrenia, rendering us uncomfortably complicit in our own erasure. This is doubly true because for women, signifiers of race and class, such as accent and grammar, are intimately linked to perceptions of femininity, sexual availability, and moral worth. A man might be working-class yet still embody the virtues of an exemplary masculinity. While working-class women are not models of exemplary femininity: we're too loud, too rough. The things we're taught to minimise about our class background contribute to our oppression as women. Well-behaved girls don't push themselves forward. Nice girls are modest and well-mannered. To be thought of as "well brought up" is to defer in discussion, to be compliant and submissive to those in positions of authority.

Working-class women are thus doubly erased: either you *can't* shake the myriad signifiers of your class background, in which case you're beneath contempt. You're not a *real* woman, so you're not, on any meaningful level, a real person. You're the punchline to a dirty joke, a cartoon, a stereotype. Either that or you front so successfully that you erase any overt signal of your class background from your daily interactions. You disappear inside the collective assumption of a middle-class default. This assumption brings with it its own specific pain: it refuses to acknowledge or account for the material conditions of your life and how these conditions impact upon your work. It is an assumption that invisiblises effort, an assumption which insists on seeing your achievements as equal to those of your middle-class colleagues.

And "equal" might sound fine, but I think we should be aiming higher than that. What both the assumption of a middle-class default, and the "representation" paradigm do, is focus on the end result: your job title, your book deal, your doctorate, etc. Neither sees the journey from point a to point b, or the endlessly proliferating series of obstacles that stood between you and your goal. That's not "equal". To succeed, however partially, inside a system set up to exclude you, is to undertake a frightening amount of extra work. You work to navigate the byzantine bureaucracies nobody told you to expect or how to negotiate. You work to meaningfully compete without the networks, leg-ups and early-stage support of your middle-class colleagues. As a working-class woman you work to balance child care and elder care and domestic responsibilities without the luxury of being able to palm this labour off onto other women lower down the socio-economic food chain, or onto labour saving devices and costly short-cuts. You work with poverty, in unconducive conditions, with the sound of your screaming neighbours through paper thin and mildew-mottled walls. You work with the concomitant effects of poverty on mental and physical health. You struggle to afford travel, books, a decent laptop, things your middle-class colleagues take for granted. And nobody ever acknowledges this. Not once. That isn't "equal".

And that's why it hurts so much when organisations and institutions point you out, as if your mere presence were evidence of how singularly inclusive they are. Especially when these same organisations have stubbornly failed to account for the material dimensions of your life, and the ways in which they adversely affect you.

Because everybody pretends not to see class, because everybody pretends not to see poverty, you minimise it too. You don't want to humiliate yourself, or appear ungreatful, or difficult, or on the scrounge. There is such absolute moral authority encoded in the notion of "hard work", of stoically putting up, shutting up, and doing for yourself, that we connive at our own invisibility. And we shouldn't. Putting together this anthology is a small push back against this invisibility. A chance to say "I hear you." A chance to say "we are here". Because celebrating ourselves and each other is important. It's one step in a long fight, but it's a significant one.

The mainstream media likes to spin the creative successes of working-class women into narratives of individual exceptionalism. A friend of mine described this process as being made into a kind of "diversity mascot". It allows cultural elites to pay lip-service to the idea of inclusivity through tokenistic acts of representation, while repositioning structural inequality as a generic and depoliticized adversity. This model of inclusion keeps us competing, and is toxic to all forms of affective solidarity.

So we're trying to clear some space here. Just a little. To carve out a bit of breathing room in the arts for ourselves, not as individuals, but as a powerful collective, a strong polyvocal "we".

Contributors

Amy Acre is a poet, performer and freelance writer from London, and the winner of the 2019 Verve Poetry Competition with 'every girl knows', which has recently been published in the Verve anthology, *Closed Gates or Open Arms*. Her pamphlet, *Where We're Going, We Don't Need Roads* (flipped eye, 2015) was chosen as a PBS Pamphlet Choice and Poetry School Best Book. She runs Bad Betty Press with Jake Wild Hall.

Deborah Alma teaches part-time at Keele University. She is editor of *Emergency Poet—an anti-stress poetry anthology, The Everyday Poet—Poems to live by* (both Michael O'Mara), *#MeToo—rallying against sexual harassment —a women's poetry anthology* (Fair Acre Press 2018) & *Ten Poems of Happiness* (Candlestick Press). Her *True Tales of the Countryside* was with The Emma Press, and her first full collection is *Dirty Laundry*, published by Nine Arches Press (2018). She runs the Poetry Pharmacy from her home town of Bishop's Castle in Shropshire.

Catherine Ayres lives and works in Northumberland. Her debut collection, *Amazon*, was published by Indigo Dreams in 2016.

Julia Bell is a writer and Reader in Creative Writing at Birkbeck, University of London, where she is the Course Director of the MA in Creative Writing. Her recent creative work includes poetry, lyric essays and short stories published in the *Paris Review, Times Literary Supplement, The White Review, Mal Journal*, Comma Press, and recorded for the BBC. She has also published three novels with Macmillan in the UK (Simon & Schuster in the US) and is the co-editor of the bestselling Creative Writing Coursebook (Macmillan) updated and re-issued in 2019. Julia is interested in the intersection between the personal and the political, and believes that writing well takes courage, patience, attention and commitment, qualities she tries to encourage in her students.

Becky Bone is a mature student, studying a Creative Writing and English BA at Birkbeck University. She began writing sporadically in 2011 through the form of stand-up comedy where she sold her soul on the London open mic scene, before joining an all-female improv group and later being one half of a sketch duo. She works part-time with children as a creative arts facilitator. Her writing, performing and work experience organically led to her decision to go back into education in 2017.

Alison Brackenbury was born in 1953. Her work has won an Eric Gregory Award and a Cholmondeley Award, and has frequently been broadcast on BBC Radio 3 and 4. *Gallop*, her Selected Poems, was published in 2019 by Carcanet. New poems can be read on her website: http://alisonbrackenbury.co.uk/

Carole Bromley lives in York where she is the Stanza rep and does poetry surgeries. Three collections from Smith/Doorstop. A fourth, *The Peregrine Falcons of York Minster*, will be published by Valley Press in 2020 and a pamphlet, *Sodium 136* due out from Calder Valley Poetry in November. Carole won the 2019 Hamish Canham Award.

Jane Burn's poems have appeared in many magazines including *The Rialto, Strix, Butcher's Dog* and *Under The Radar*, and anthologies from publishers such as Seren and The Emma Press. Since 2014, her poems have had success in 42 poetry competitions. Her pamphlets include *Fat Around the Middle* (Talking Pen, 2015) and *Tongues of Fire* (BLERoom, 2016), and her collections are *nothing more to it than bubbles* (Indigo Dreams, 2016), *This Game of Strangers* (Wyrd Harvest Press, 2017 co-written with Bob Beagrie), *One of These Dead Places* (Culture Matters), Fleet (Wyrd Harvest Press), *Remnants* (Knives Forks and Spoons Press, co-written with Bob Beagrie) and *Yan, Tan, Tether* (Indigo Dreams, 2020). Her poems have been nominated for the Forward and Pushcart Prize. Jane Burn is an Associate Editor at Culture Matters.

Kimberly Campanello's poetry books and pamphlets include *Consent, Imagines, Strange Country* (on the sheela-na-gig stone carvings), and *Hymn to Kālī* (her version of the Karpūrādi-stotra). In April 2019, zimZalla released *MOTHERBABYHOME*, a 796-page poetry-object and reader's edition book comprising conceptual and visual poetry on the St Mary's Mother and Baby Home in Tuam, Ireland. Also in April, above / ground press published her chapbook running commentary along the bottom of the tapestry. She was recently awarded a 2019 Markievicz Bursary from Ireland's Arts Council and the Department of Culture, Heritage and the Gaeltacht for her (S)worn State(s), a poetry collaboration with Dimitra Xidous and Annemarie Ní Churreáin. She is Programme Leader for Creative Writing and a member of the Poetry Centre in the School of English at the University of Leeds.

Geraldine Clarkson lives and works in Warwickshire. A teacher of English to refugees and migrants, she has also worked in care homes, warehouses, libraries and offices, and spent time in a silent monastic order, including some years in South America. She has published poetry pamphlets with smith|doorstop (2016) and Shearsman Books (2016, 2018).

Jo Clement is Managing Editor of *Butcher's Dog* poetry magazine and co-edits *Multiples*, the journal of the Society of Wood Engravers. In 2012 she received a New Writing North Award selected by Paul Farley. Her poems have been shortlisted for the Bridport, Melita Hulme and Troubadour International prizes. Jo holds a practice-led PhD in Creative Writing from Newcastle University, which was awarded an inaugural AHRC Northern Bridge scholarship. *Outlandish* (New Writing North, 2019) is an Arts Council England-supported poetry pamphlet made in collaboration with the writer Damian Le Bas and the artist W. John Hewitt. It explores the changing landscape of Gypsy identity through walking, drawing and writing: joclement.co.uk

Rachael Clyne, from Glastonbury, is a psychotherapist who has published self-help books. Her poetry collection concerns our relationship with nature and she is passionate about eco-issues. Her recent pamphlet, *Girl Golem* (4Word Press) explores her Jewish migrant background (both her parents migrated as toddlers from Ukrainian Russia). Her sense of being other, culturally and sexually, is a strong theme in her work. Her poems appear in a range of journals and she enjoys reading at poetry events.

Jane Commane was born in Coventry and lives and works in Warwickshire. Her first full-length collection, *Assembly Lines*, was published by Bloodaxe in 2018. Her poetry has featured in anthologies including *The Best British Poetry 2011* (Salt Publishing) and *Lung Jazz: Young British Poets for Oxfam* (Cinnamon), and in magazines including *Anon, And Other Poems, Bare Fiction, Iota, Tears in the Fence* and *The North*. In 2016, she was chosen to join Writing West Midlands' Room 204 writer development programme. Jane is editor at Nine Arches Press, co-editor of *Under the Radar* magazine, organiser of the WordPlay poetry series in Coventry, and is co-author (with Jo Bell) of *How to Be a Poet*, a creative writing handbook and blog series. In 2017 she was awarded a Jerwood Compton Poetry Fellowship.

Michelle Diaz has been writing poetry since the late 90s. She started reading her poems at the Poetry Café in Covent Garden in 1999. She has been widely published both online and in print. Her debut pamphlet *The Dancing Boy* was published in 2019 with Against the Grain Poetry Press. Without poetry her soul would be incredibly hungry.

Imtiaz Dharker is a poet, artist and video film-maker. She was awarded the Queen's Gold Medal for Poetry in 2014. A Fellow of the Royal Society of Literature, she has been Poet-in-Residence at Cambridge University Library and has worked on several projects across art forms in Leeds, Newcastle and Hull, as well as the Archives of St Paul's Cathedral. Her six collections include

Over the Moon and the latest, Luck Is the Hook, all published by Bloodaxe Books UK, and her poems have been broadcast widely on BBC Radio 3 and 4 as well as the BBC World Service. She has had eleven solo exhibitions of drawings around the world, and scripts and directs video films, many of them for non-government organisations working in the area of shelter, education and health for women and children in India.

Sarah Doyle is the Pre-Raphaelite Society's Poet-in-Residence, and is co-author (with Allen Ashley) of *Dreaming Spheres: Poems of the Solar System* (PS Publishing, 2014). She holds an MA in Creative Writing from Royal Holloway College, University of London, and has been published widely in magazines, journals and anthologies. She won first prize in the WoLF Poetry Competition and Holland Park Press's Brexit in Poetry 2019; was a runner-up in the Keats-Shelley Poetry Prize 2019; and was highly commended in the Ginkgo Prize for Ecopoetry and in the Best Single Poem category of the Forward Prizes 2018. She is co-editor (again, with Allen Ashley) of *Humanagerie*, an anthology of animal-inspired poetry and fiction, published by Eibonvale Press in 2018. Sarah is currently researching a PhD in the poetics of meteorology at Birmingham City University. Her website is at: www.sarahdoyle.co.uk

Nadia Drews was born in San Francisco and brought up in Greater Manchester. A Socialist mother with a suitcase of vinyl recordings by Leadbelly and Howlin' Wolf and a well-earned Young Democrats badge led her to revolutionary politics and eventually to sing and write songs about changing the world, first in the bedroom and then on stage. The stories of working-class lives in the songs grew into plays and she left Manchester having written and co-produced 'I Love Vinegar Vera (What Becomes of the Brokenhearted)' based on the local legend of a woman that each Lancashire town seemed to have. Having moved closer to family roots in the East End of London in 2011 she began to perform poetry at the Poetry Cafe's Poetry Unplugged night and then to become a Farrago Poetry Slam champion. Through this she has been able to find the ranting voice she was unable to achieve in the 80's. Thirty years of repressed rhymes mean she writes long poems... but she reads them fast.

Cathy Dreyer is a poet and critic who lives in Oxfordshire. She is a founder member of Poets for the Planet and has an MPhil in Creative Writing.

Carrie Etter has published four collections of poetry, most recently *Imagined Sons* (Seren, 2014), shortlisted for the Ted Hughes Award for New Work in Poetry, and *The Weather in Normal* (UK: Seren; US: Station Hill, 2018), a Poetry Book Society Recommendation. She is Reader in Creative Writing at Bath Spa University and also teaches for The Poetry School and Poetry Swindon.

Sally Flint grew up in the West Midlands and now lives in Exeter. Her poetry and prose have been widely published, anthologised and won awards. She teaches creative writing, facilitates community workshops and is co-founder/editor of Riptide short story journal and Canto Poetry at the University of Exeter. She also works with Devon Drugs Service and Devon Community Foundation on a project 'Stories Connect', based on the University of Massachusetts' programme, 'Changing Lives through Literature.' Her research interests include healthcare in the arts, and the evolution of ekphrasis, especially the relationship between poetry, visual art and technology.

Novelist, poet and singer with post-punk band The March Violets, **Rosie Garland** has a passion for language nurtured by public libraries. Her work's appeared in *Under the Radar, The North, Rialto, Mslexia* & elsewhere. Rosie is the author of three novels: *The Palace of Curiosities, Vixen*, and *The Night Brother. The Times* has described her writing as "a delight: playful and exuberant." http://www.rosiegarland.com/

Raine Geoghegan, MA is of Romany Heritage. She writes poetry, monologues and short prose. Her debut pamphlet, *Apple Water: Povel Panni* from Hedgehog Press was launched in December 2019 and previewed at the Ledbury Poetry Festival. Her poetry has been nominated for the Pushcart Prize, Best of the Net and the Forward Prize. *Apple Water* was chosen as a spring 2019 Selection by the Poetry Book Society. Publications include: *Under the Radar; Poetry Ireland Review; The Travellers' Times* and many more.

Jackie Hagan is a working-class, queer amputee with systemic sclerosis and bipolar. She is a Jerwood Compton Poetry Fellow and a multi award-winning playwright, poet and stand-up comedian. She is passionate about accessibility in the widest sense and in us making the world a better place by shrugging off conventions that are just nasty hangovers from the past.

Nicki Heinen is published in magazines and anthologies, including *Magma* and Bad Betty Press' recent *The Dizziness of Freedom*. She founded and hosts Words & Jazz, a poetry and music night at the Vortex Jazz Club, Dalston. Her debut pamphlet *Itch* is out now with Eyewear Publishing, and was an LRB Bookshop Book of the Year.

Julie Hogg is published in many literary journals including *Abridged, Black Light Engine Room, Butcher's Dog, Corrugated Wave, Honest Ulsterman, Irisi, Poethead, Popshot, Proletarian Poetry, Well Versed* and *Words for the Wild*. Featured in anthologies by Listen Softly, Litmus, Zoomorphic and Seren, her debut pamphlet *Majuba Road* is available from Vane Women Press.

Maya Horton is an artist, writer and astronomer currently based in the South East of England. Her pamphlet *The Valley of Winter* was published by the Black Light Engine Room Press (2019). She is the editor of *Until the Stars Burn Out*, a twice-annual arts and poetry magazine devoted to astronomy. She was raised in a small closed religious group and writes about this often.

Helen Ivory is a poet and visual artist. She edits the webzine *Ink Sweat and Tears*, and is a lecturer for the UEA/National Centre for Writing online creative writing programme. Her fifth collection from Bloodaxe Books, *The Anatomical Venus*, examines how women have been portrayed as 'other'; as witches; as hysterics with wandering wombs and as beautiful corpses cast in wax, or on mortuary slabs in TV box sets, was published in 2019. It was shortlisted for the East Anglian Book Awards and won the East Anglian Writers 'Book by the Cover Award'. A book of collage/mixed media poems, *Hear What the Moon Told Me*, was published KFS in 2017, and a chapbook, *Maps of the Abandoned City*, by SurVision in 2019. She lives in Norwich. Her website is www.helenivory.co.uk.

Carolyn Jess-Cooke is a poet and novelist published in 23 languages. Her latest novel is *THE NESTING* (HarperCollins, 2020). She is Senior Lecturer in Creative Writing at the University of Glasgow.

Lisa Kelly's first collection, *A Map Towards Fluency*, was published by Carcanet in June. Her poems have appeared in *Stairs and Whispers: D/deaf and Disabled Poets Write Back* (Nine Arches Press) and Carcanet's *New Poetries VII*. Her pamphlets are *Philip Levine's Good Ear* (Stonewood Press) and *Bloodhound* (Hearing Eye). Lisa is Chair of *Magma Poetry* and often hosts poetry events at the Torriano Meeting House, London—a grassroots community arts venue. She is currently studying British Sign Language and is a freelance journalist.

Joanne Key lives in Cheshire. She is completely in love with poetry and short stories and writes every day. Her work has been published in various places both online and in print. She has won prizes in a number of competitions including second prize in both the National Poetry Competition in 2014 and The Charles Causley Competition in 2016. She was Runner-Up in the Prole Poetry Competition in 2017. In 2018 she won the Hippocrates Open Prize. Her poems have also been commended or highly commended in a number of other competitions and she has been previously shortlisted for *Mslexia*, the Plough, Winchester, the National Poetry Competition and the Bridport Prize. She was the winner of the 2018 Mslexia Short Story Competition.

Laura Lawson is a writer and prize-winning painter who lives on her beloved Northumberland Coast with her husband and two daughters. Her poetry has been published in the Dark Matter pamphlet series by Black Light Engine Room and various literary magazines in print and online. She has worked on a number of interdisciplinary projects that embrace the crossover of literature and the visual arts in constant rebellion to her Fine Art Degree where she was told that she had to keep her writing separate.

Melissa Lee-Houghton was born in Wythenshawe, Manchester. She was named a Next Generation Poet 2014 following her second collection, *Beautiful Girls*, which was a Poetry Book Society Recommendation. Her most recent book of poetry, *Sunshine*, was published by Penned in the Margins in 2016 and saw her shortlisted for the Costa Poetry Award, Ted Hughes Award and Forward Prize for Best Single Poem. In 2017 she was awarded a Somerset Maugham Award by the Society of Authors.

Pippa Little is Scots and lives in Northumberland. She is a poet, editor, mentor and workshop facilitator and is currently working on a third full collection and a pamphlet.

Fran Lock is a sometime itinerant dog-whisperer and the author of seven poetry collections, most recently *Raptures and Captures* (Culture Matters, 2019) in collaboration with collage artist Steev Burgess, and *Contains Mild Peril* (Out-Spoken Press, 2019). She is an associate editor at Culture Matters, and has recently submitted her Ph.D. at Birkbeck College University of London. Her poetry is concerned with the unlikely strategies for resistance in the day to day struggles of working-class women and girls, and with exposing the half-hidden histories of working-class lives.

Hannah Lowe's latest book is *The Neighbourhood* (Outspoken 2019).

Kirsten Luckins is a writer and performer from the north-east. She has toured two spoken word theatre shows with Arts Council support, and her collection *The Trouble With Compassion* (Burning Eye) was launched at StAnza Festival in 2016. She has work in many magazines, including *Under The Radar*, *Butcher's Dog*, *The Interpreter's House*, and *Magma*.

Char March is a poet, playwright, fiction writer, tutor, and creative coach. She is author of five poetry collections, six BBC Radio 4 plays, nine stage plays, two screenplays and a collection of 13 of her award-winning short stories. She has been Writer-in-Residence for Leeds Hospitals, for European Business Schools, Temple Newsam Mansion, NHS Research, Ty Newydd, Care Homes in North Yorkshire, and the National Midwives' Conference. She works as a tutor, an editor for publishers, and an editor/mentor for individual writers. Her fifth poetry collection is just published: https://www.valleypressuk.com/book/105/full_stops_in_winter_branches.

Lisa Matthews is a prose/experimental poet currently writing up her Ph.D. thesis exploring text blocks and sequentiality; her fourth collection, *Callisto* (Red Squirrel Press), is in its second edition, and you can see a selection of Lisa's work-in-progress at TextBlockCentral (www.textblockcentral.eu).

Beth McDonough's work connects strongly with place, particularly to the Tay, where she swims, foraging nearby. Her poetry is published in *Gutter, Stand, Agenda, Poetry Salzburg Review* and elsewhere. She reviews at *DURA*. *Handfast* (with Ruth Aylett, Mother's Milk Books, 2016) is a verse investigation of family experiences of autism and dementia. Her first solo pamphlet, *Lamping for pickled fish*, was published in September 2019 by 4Word Books.

AJ McKenna has done a bunch of stuff: two pamphlets (*A Lady of a Certain Rage* and *names and songs of women*), a novella (*Incidents of Trespass*), a film (*Letter to a Minnesota Prison*) and a one-woman show (*Howl of the Bantee*) which has been presented in Edinburgh and London. As part of Apples and Snakes' 2015 Public Address tour, she created *Shotgun Wedding*, a hybrid performance poetry/performance art piece in which audiences were required to attack her with dry rice and water pistols, which was quite exciting. She currently spends her time developing her second one-woman show, *Struggle/Play* and trying, largely unsuccessfully, to get better at YouTube.

Rosemary McLeish is an artist and poet aged 73 now living in Kent. She has had poems published in various anthologies and magazines, and her first collection, *I Am A Field* came out in February 2019. In December 2017, after two earlier skirmishes with breast cancer (and two mastectomies), she was diagnosed with Stage 4 breast cancer in her spine.

Jessica Mookherjee is a poet of Bengali origin. She grew up in Wales and now lives in Kent. She has been published in many print and online journals including *Agenda, Interpreter's House, The North, Rialto, Under the Radar* and *Antiphon*. She has two pamphlets, *The Swell* (TellTale Press) and *Joyride* (BLER Press). She was highly commended for best single poem in the Forward Prize 2017. Her first collection is *Flood* (2018, Cultured Llama) and her second, *Tigress* is published by Nine Arches Press. She is co-editor of Against the Grain Poetry Press.

Kim Moore's first collection *The Art of Falling* (Seren, 2015) won the 2016 Geoffrey Faber Memorial Prize. She won a Northern Writers Award in 2014, an Eric Gregory Award in 2011 and the Geoffrey Dearmer Prize in 2010. Her pamphlet *If We Could Speak Like Wolves* was a winner in the 2012 Poetry Business Pamphlet Competition. She is currently a PhD candidate at Manchester Metropolitan University and is working on her second collection. She is Co-Director of Kendal Poetry Festival.

Katrina Naomi's third full collection, *Wild Persistence*, is due from Seren in June 2020. Her most recent pamphlet, *Typhoon Etiquette*, was published in 2019 by Verve Poetry Press. It was inspired by her trip to Japan on an Arts Council-funded project. In 2018 she received a BBC commission for National Poetry Day. Her poetry has appeared in the *TLS, Poetry London, Poetry Review* and *Modern Poetry in Translation*, as well as on P*oems on the Underground*. She was shortlisted for the 2017 Forward Prize for Poetry. Her work has appeared on BBC TV and Radio 4's *Front Row* and *Poetry Please*. Her most recent collection, *The Way the Crocodile Taught Me* (Seren, 2016), was chosen by Foyles' Bookshop as one of its #FoylesFive for poetry. Katrina was the first writer-in-residence at the Brontë Parsonage Museum in W Yorks, since then she has been poet-in-residence at the Arnolfini, Gladstone's Library and the Leach Pottery. She has a PhD in Creative Writing (Goldsmiths) and tutors for Arvon, Ty Newydd and the Poetry School: www.katrinanaomi.co.uk

Golnoosh Nour has read in numerous literary events across the UK and internationally, including at the Stoke Newington Literary Festival, The Suffle at the Poetry Café, and Isn't Everything Poetry? in Berlin. Her debut poetry collection, *Sorrows of the Sun*, was published by Skyscraper in 2017. Her short story collection, *The Ministry of Guidance and other Stories*, is due for publication in April 2020. For more info, visit her website: golnooshwriter. weebly.com

Hibaq Osman is a Somali writer born and based in London. Her work largely centers women, identity and the healing process with a focus on the often hidden, nuanced aspects of our experiences. Her debut poetry collection, *A Silence You Can Carry*, was published with Out-Spoken Press in 2015. In 2017 she released her online poetry chapbook the heart is a smashed bulb.

Abigail Parry's first collection, *Jinx*, is published by Bloodaxe, and deals in trickery, gameplay, masks and costume. The poems have won a number of awards, including the Ballymaloe Prize, the Troubadour Prize and an Eric Gregory Award.

Ellen Phethean worked with Julia Darling in The Poetry Virgins, and they set up Diamond Twig Press. Ellen wrote *Wall*, a teen novel in poems, published by Smokestack Books 2007. Her first collection of poetry, *Breath*, 2009 was shortlisted for the London Fringe 1st Collection Award 2010, her second collection, *Portrait of the Quince as an Older Woman* (2014) was a New Writing North Read Regional Selection. Her YA novel *Ren and the Blue Hands* was published in 2016. The next two, *Ren and the Blue Cloth* and *Ren In Samara*, were published December 2019, all by Red Squirrel Press. She runs workshops and teaches Creative Writing and lives in Newcastle upon Tyne.

Kathy Pimlott's two pamphlets, *Elastic Glue* (2019) and *Goose Fair Night* (2016), were both published by The Emma Press. Her poems have appeared a variety of anthologies, including *Second Place Rosette* (ed. Richard O'Brien and Emma Wright), *Vaster Than Empires* (ed. Joy Howard), *One For the Road* (ed. Helen Mort), *Urban Myths and Legends* (ed. Rachel Piercey and Emma Wright), and *Best Friends Forever* (ed. Amy Key). Born in Nottingham, in the shadow of Player's cigarette factory, she has spent her adult life in Covent Garden. She has been, among other things, a social worker and community activist and currently works on community-led public realm projects. www.kathypimlott.co.uk @kathy_pimlott

Wendy Pratt is an award-winning poet and freelance writer living on the glorious North Yorkshire coast. She is the coastal columnist for Yorkshire Life magazine and editor of literary arts magazine *Dream Catcher*. Her latest collection, *When I Think of My Body as a Horse*, will be published by Valley Press in 2020.

Lesley Quayle is a poet, an editor and folk/blues singer. Her work has appeared widely in poetry magazines, including *The Rialto, Tears in the Fence and The North*, also *The Spectator, Morning Star, Yorkshire Post, Yorkshire Journal*, local radio and BBC Radio 4. Her poem 'Termination' was nominated for a Forward Prize. Her pamphlet *Songs For Lesser Gods*, featuring the prizewinning sonnet sequence of the same title, was published by erbacce in 2010, and in 2013, Indigo Dreams published her collection, *Sessions*. Her recent pamphlet, *Black Bicycle*, was published by 4Word.

Legna Rodríguez Iglesias was born in Camagüey, Cuba in 1984. She works in a variety of genres, including poetry, short stories, novels, children's books and theatre. She has won a number of prestigious national and international prizes; most recently she was awarded the Premio Paz in 2016 in Miami for her collection of poems, *Miami Century Fox*.

Clare Saponia is a London-born, Berlin-based writer, linguist and multidisciplinary artist. Her first collection, *Copywriting War and other Business Sins* (Olympia Publishers) was published in 2011, followed by a second, *The Oranges of Revolution* (Smokestack Books) in April 2015. Her work has appeared in a wide range of magazines and anthologies including: *Emergency Verse—Poetry in Defence of the Welfare State* (Caparison 2011), *The Robin Hood Book—Verse Versus Austerity* (Caparison 2012) and *Kakania —An Anthology* (Austrian Cultural Forum 2015).

Jacqueline Saphra's *The Kitchen of Lovely Contraptions* (flipped eye 2011) was shortlisted for the Aldeburgh First Collection Prize. *If I Lay on my Back I Saw Nothing but Naked Women* (The Emma Press 2014) won the Saboteur Award for Best Collaborative Work. *A Bargain with the Light: Poems after Lee Miller* was published by Hercules Editions in 2017 and in the same year *All My Mad Mothers* (Nine Arches Press) was shortlisted for the T.S. Eliot prize. Her most recent collection is *Dad, Remember You are Dead* from Nine Arches Press.

Pauline Sewards helps run a monthly spoken word event in Bristol called Satelite of Love. Her first poetry collection, *This is the Band*, was published by Hearing Eye in 2018, and she has a new collection to be published by Burning Eye Books in 2020. In 2019 she was co-editor of *Magma* 74 on the theme of 'Work'.

Clare Shaw has three poetry collections from Bloodaxe: *Straight Ahead* (2006), *Head On* (2012), and *Flood* (2018). Often addressing political and personal conflict, her poetry is fuelled by a strong conviction in the transformative and redemptive power of language. Clare is an Associate Fellow with the Royal Literary Fund, and a regular tutor for the Poetry School, the Wordsworth Trust and the Arvon Foundation. She won a Northern Writer's Award 2018, and was a judge for the Ted Hughes Prize 2018.

Natalie Shaw has a kind husband and children of varying sizes. She was commended in the 2018 National poetry Competition. Her pamphlet *Oh be quiet* will be published in 2020 by Against the Grain Press.

My name is **Hannah Shelmerdine**. I am a severely disabled lady, living with Cerebral Palsy. My story entitled, *The Red Admiral Butterfly*, explains how my life has been transformed through the appearance of the Red Admiral Butterfly. I believe that this is a sign of spiritual guidance from my deceased grandparents, through which they made their presence known, sending me these beautiful butterflies as a constant reminder that they're never far away and will remain with me forever. The butterflies have given me the strength I needed to overcome depression, enabling me to find life fulfillment. I am now an extreme sportswoman and adventurer.

Natalie Sirett's practice is concerned with female icons in contemporary culture, fairytale and myth, from Eve and Pandora to Drag Kings and Barbie Brides. Working in a range of media, including paint, printmaking and textiles, Natalie has exhibited widely in the UK, most recently at Burgh House Museum and The Diorama Arts Centre, both in London. She is involved in collaborations with writers including Medusa & Her Sisters, a limited edition book with fourteen contemporary poets, published October 2019, and Okoro with the award-winning author Sita Brahmachari, to be published in 2021. Natalie trained in Fine Art at Newcastle University and the Royal Academy Schools. She lives and works in London.

Mary Lou Springstead is a visual artist who specialises in painting. Her art explores myth, soul, humanity, nature, politics and humour. Her influences are Expressionism, Surrealism, Feminist Art, Outsider Art and Lowbrow Art. She currently lives in Middlesbrough with her husband p.a. morbid, poet and editor of The Black Light Engine Room Press. Please visit her artist website: marylouspringstead.com.

Joelle Taylor is an award-winning poet, playwright and author currently touring her latest collection *Songs My Enemy Taught Me* across the UK, Europe, and Australia. She is the founder of the Poetry Society's national youth slams SLAMbassadors, and the host of Out-Spoken.

Angela Topping has had eight full collections and four pamphlets out with reputable publishers. Her work has featured on BBC Radio *Poetry Please*, and in over 100 anthologies, in journals including *Poetry Review, The Dark Horse* and *Magma*. She is a former Writer-in-Residence at Gladstone's Library.

Denni Turp is a Welsh-speaking Cockney writer in rural north Wales, a green Socialist, a staunch republican since her early teens, a dog rehomer, and a woman with a very long working life (mostly in the not-for-profit community sector) behind her. As part of the annual global initiative 100 Thousand Poets for Change, she has organised the north Wales event with poets and musicians for the last 5 years. Her poems have been published in a number of magazines and webzines and the occasional anthology.

Serafina Vick graduated from King's College London in 2015 with a First Class degree in French and Hispanic Studies. She started translating Cuban poetry in 2014 whilst studying in Havana. Her translations have been featured in *Modern Poetry in Translation* and *Bogota 39*, and on BBC Radio 4. She lives in Havana, where she's currently working on her first novel.

Julia Webb grew up on a council estate in Thetford in rural Norfolk. She left school at 16 and came to studying late. She has a poetry MA from the University of East Anglia. Her first collection, *Bird Sisters*, was published by Nine Arches Press in 2016. Her second collection, *Threat*, was published in by Nine Arches in 2019.

Ten years ago, **Sarah Wedderburn** left London to live above the marsh in East Kent. Since then, her poems have appeared in various publications in print and online. She studied English at Oxford, holds a Poetry School MA, and has a career as a writer on art and architecture. She misses her lurcher companion and is currently walking retired greyhounds.